ALIGN PRESS

6 Glenn Gould Crescent
Uxbridge, Ontario, Canada L9P1W4

COPYRIGHT © 2024 NANCIE EVANS, PHD
Published by Align Press, a division of Culture-Strategy Fit Inc.

ISBN
eBook: 978-1-7381717-0-5
Paperback: 978-1-7381717-2-9
Hardcover: 978-1-7381717-1-2

First Edition
Book Production and Publishing by Brands Through Books
brandsthroughbooks.com

https://www.culturestrategyfit.com

Where Culture *Meets* *Strategy*

How to Solve Problems,
Change Behavior,
and Lead Your Team
to Success

Nancie Evans, PhD

ALIGN
PRESS

This book is dedicated to my husband and life partner, Alan Risen, and my friend and colleague Sherrill Burns for their unwavering support and encouragement. Thank you for believing in me. This book would not have been possible without you.

CONTENTS

PRIVACY STATEMENT

While the stories shared in this book are true, names and details have been changed to protect the identities of individuals and organizations.

INTRODUCTION

IF YOU'VE PICKED UP THIS BOOK, you are probably a human resource (HR) or organization development (OD) professional searching for a better way to help your organization build or change its culture. You have probably tried training programs, culture survey action plans, values initiatives, and other approaches and are dissatisfied with the results. You may even be looking for a way to convince senior leaders to take a more active role in the work of building the culture your organization needs. If this is the case, I have good news.

There is a better way. A way to intentionally build and change culture that is owned and led by leaders with the support of HR/OD, not owned and led by HR/OD with the support of leaders. A pragmatic, results-oriented approach where leaders apply their critical thinking abilities, problem-solving skills, and business knowledge to align culture with strategy, solve culture problems, and create great organizations with great cultures.

Are you interested and maybe even a bit excited? If so, this book is for you. It shows you how to engage leaders so they personally own and are actively involved in building and changing culture; how to solve culture problems that are interfering with strategy execution and performance; and, ultimately, how to intentionally build the culture your organization needs to thrive. It answers the question, "How do we achieve meaningful and sustainable culture change in organizations?"

This book is the culmination of my thirty-five years of research and experience partnering with HR/OD leaders and their teams to conduct culture assessments and design and implement culture change initiatives. It draws on the lessons I have learned and insights I have gained from working with over a hundred small and large organizations across a wide range of industries, sectors, and geographies. It is informed by the knowledge I gained from my doctoral studies, when I first had the opportunity to observe a significant culture change happen in only four months. It was this experience that truly ignited my passion for this work and my desire to share what I have learned with other professionals like you who want to do meaningful culture work.

THE CULTURE FIELD TODAY

Organizations spend millions of dollars annually on culture assessments and culture change initiatives, with much of the investment going to consultants for training, workshops, and surveys. Why do they do this?

Leaders recognize that culture is important and are willing to invest in it. In fact, a 2021 report by the consulting firm PricewaterhouseCoopers reported that 66 percent of C-suite executives and board members believe culture is more important than a company's strategy or operating model.[1] Yet, it is estimated that only 30 percent of culture change efforts deliver the results companies need, according to a 2019 report in the *Harvard Business Review*.[2] Why is this happening?

It is certainly not from a lack of attention and study. In fact, the concept of organizational culture and culture change first caught the attention of business leaders in the early 1980s and can be linked to the release of Allan Kennedy and Terrence Deal's book *Corporate Cultures: The Rites and Rituals of Corporate Life*. It was Kennedy and Deal who coined the oft-used definition of organizational culture, "the way we do things around here," which remains popular to this day.[3] This work was quickly followed by several other influential books, such as Peter Senge's *The Fifth Discipline* (1990), Jim Collins's *Good to Great* (2001), and John Kotter and James Heskett's *Corporate Culture and Performance* (1992). All these books argue that a company's culture directly impacts its performance and is a potential source of competitive differentiation. Importantly, they also argue that managing culture is one of the most important roles of a leader.

So, what is the problem?

If there is one thing I learned early on that has never changed, it is that leadership, specifically the words and actions of people in positions of influence, is the single most important factor in determining the success of culture alignment and change efforts. This refers specifically to people who hold senior management positions, because of the scope and scale of influence they have on the way things happen in an organization. This influence is not limited to acting as role models of the required behaviors, although this is important. It is much more. It is about leaders personally owning and actively participating in the intentional effort of building and changing culture. Yet, in my experience, this rarely happens, and it is not because leaders don't care or don't think culture is important. In most cases, the opposite is true.

The reality is that leaders are faced with a constant barrage of competing demands for their time and attention. Most find themselves in back-to-back meetings, leaving little time to do "real work" except perhaps in the evenings and on weekends, and even this is often spent getting ready for the next stream of meetings. They are forced to make choices regarding where they invest their time, and often, culture gets delegated, usually to the HR function. After all, culture is about people and their behavior, so who better to own culture change than HR?

Unfortunately, this is a major reason why culture change efforts fail. You see, it is the leader, not HR, who makes decisions every day that directly affect the way the people in their organization and team interact and go about their work. These decisions, which include how they show up with others (behaviors), are based on their beliefs as to the best and right way to do things. These beliefs, and the decisions and actions they are based on, are what build culture. Take, for example, a leader who believes the best way to achieve the outcomes the company needs is to be process-oriented. To this end, the leader decides to invest in Six Sigma and Lean manufacturing to reduce waste and minimize defects. This requires new skills and knowledge, redesigned processes, new techniques, new tools, different roles and responsibilities, new practices, and different behavior, among other things. By acting on his beliefs, the leader takes steps toward building a process-oriented culture, whether he knows it or not.

This is not to say the HR function doesn't play an important role, because it does. In fact, HR controls several of the most powerful levers for building culture, including recognition and rewards systems, organization design, and hiring and selection criteria. In this example, HR may assist with job design, conduct job evaluations for new roles, provide communication and change management support, source training programs, or perhaps assist with hiring people with the needed skills and experience. They might even provide counseling and coaching on how to build a process-oriented culture; however, they cannot do everything for the leader. Of course, senior HR leaders are also in positions of influence, and therefore, through their beliefs and actions, build the culture within their function and team and play an important role in shaping the culture of the organization. The point is that building and changing culture cannot be delegated, period.

The only way culture change is successful is when leaders own it and are actively involved in making it happen. Yet, in my experience, it is rare that a senior leader stands up and says, "We need to change our culture, and I am personally going to make this happen." Instead, most leaders turn to HR/OD and outside experts and ask us what we are going to do. This must change.

There is a solution.

We need to do things differently. We HR/OD profession-als need to offer leaders a different way to think about culture, their roles, and how they can create a culture by design versus default. We need to offer them a solution that clearly shows them how building and changing culture is not something new or complex. As leaders, they do it every day, although they may not realize it. Furthermore, they likely already have some of the skills required to tackle culture building and change, including critical thinking, problem-solving, and personal reflection.

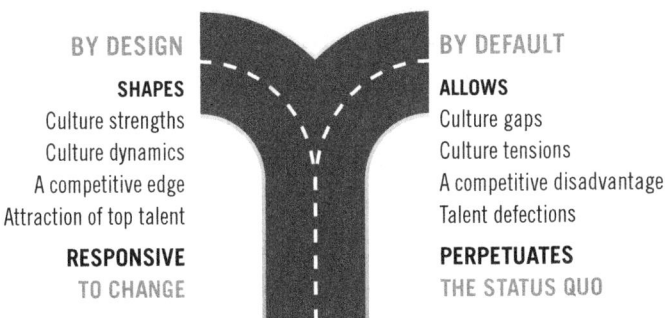

BY DESIGN	BY DEFAULT
SHAPES	**ALLOWS**
Culture strengths	Culture gaps
Culture dynamics	Culture tensions
A competitive edge	A competitive disadvantage
Attraction of top talent	Talent defections
RESPONSIVE	**PERPETUATES**
TO CHANGE	THE STATUS QUO

An intentional approach to culture helps organizations execute strategy, achieve goals, and provide a great place to work

Diagram 1: Culture by design

The solution I am talking about is the CASPE culture change process I developed and use in my consulting practice, which I am sharing for the first time in this book. CASPE is an acronym for *clarify, analyze, solve, pilot,* and *expand*. It works because it focuses leaders' attention on solving a business problem that is caused by the culture, not on changing the culture. For example, perhaps a company is suffering from quality issues and waste that is driving up costs due to a lack of collaboration between engineering and production. Or maybe there is redundancy and duplicated effort in new product development because business units aren't coordinating their efforts.

In many cases, leaders recognize that, to solve the problem, employees need to work and behave differently. They may even identify the new behaviors and communicate these to employees. Unfortunately, telling people to behave differently is not an effective way to achieve meaningful or sustainable change. Hence, at some point, leaders will realize they need help and turn to HR/OD. If the leaders retain ownership and are actively involved in the change effort, then great. However, if leaders abdicate their responsibility to HR/OD, we have a problem. **Culture change initiatives owned and led by HR/OD are rarely, if ever, effective at solving the problem the company is facing or at changing the culture in a meaningful way.** Instead, we need to convince leaders the solution is not to launch a culture change initiative but to focus on the changes needed to solve the specific business problem. For example, to drive collaboration, one solution might be to create an integrated team to explore the potential of AI for new product development. But first, we must understand the problem and why employees are behaving the way they are. Then, we must identify the changes required to encourage and sustain different behaviors (i.e., structures, processes, policies, procedures, physical space, etc.). This requires that the leader take the lead and be actively involved in the change effort since the leader knows the business best, understands what is feasible, and is accountable for solving the problem.

By starting with a business problem that can only be solved by changing the culture, culture change is viewed as a critical business priority, elevating it to the same level of importance and urgency as other priorities demanding leaders' time and attention. However, while leaders have many skills and abilities, culture change is rarely one of them. They need a clear, straightforward approach, which the CASPE culture change process provides, plus guidance, coaching, and support provided by you, the HR/OD professional.

HR/OD PROFESSIONALS—STRATEGIC PARTNERS IN CULTURE CHANGE

Your role as an HR/OD professional is to be a strategic partner, advising, supporting, and guiding the leader through the culture change process to achieve the outcomes the organization needs. In addition to educating leaders, at a minimum, you can facilitate or, even better, cofacilitate meetings and workshops, allowing the leader to participate more fully in discussions. By seeing the leader in action, you can also provide feedback and coaching not just on the leader's facilitation skills but, more importantly, on their behavior and how this influences others' behavior and shapes the culture.

In addition, culture change can create anxiety and trigger resistance. To prevent this from happening, the organization needs effective change management, employee communication, and engagement strategies. This includes skills training as well as, on occasion, interventions to improve team effectiveness and resolve interpersonal conflicts. Once again, it is you, the HR/OD professional, who has the skills and knowledge to address this need.

As mentioned previously, you also have control over many of the levers used to create the conditions that support and encourage new behaviors. For example, one of the most powerful motivators for behavior is compensation and total rewards. If we want to encourage collaboration but we reward individual achievements, we have a problem. Similarly, if we want business entities to collaborate on new product development and sales but design them to operate independently, we have a problem. For the culture to change, you need to be on the journey with leaders, using the tools only HR/OD professionals have to ensure the change effort is successful. All of this is explored in greater depth throughout this book, which is full of insights, ideas, tips, and techniques specifically designed to help you optimize your effectiveness as a strategic partner in culture change.

Of course, not all HR departments have the capacity or the capability to do all these things. Smaller organizations or those who outsource HR/OD often must tap into outside resources for assistance. If this is the case in your organization, then you can still add value by introducing CASPE to leaders, connecting them with the right people, and supporting them on the journey.

THE STRUCTURE OF THIS BOOK

This book is structured in three parts. In part one, I briefly cover a few important concepts before diving into the topic of culture alignment and change. This includes a short exploration of what every leader and HR/OD professional needs to know about culture and leading culture change. I also share a story about an interaction I had with a senior leader that explains how I came to realize we need to think about and approach culture change differently than the way I and other experts were previously advocating. In part two, we begin by examining the dynamics of culture drag and culture-strategy alignment. This is followed by a deep dive into the five-step CASPE culture change process, which includes examples taken from my experience working with senior leaders as they solved the culture problems their organizations faced. Finally, we conclude in part three with suggestions on how to accelerate the culture change effort and make it sustainable for the long term.

Ultimately, my hope is that this book provides you, the HR/OD leader or professional, with a way to inspire and help leaders take personal ownership of building great cultures, places where people and the company grow and thrive. The good news is that this goal is within the reach of every leader to achieve. All they need is the know-how and commitment to make it happen.

PART ONE

ORGANIZATIONAL CULTURE AND CULTURE CHANGE

CHAPTER ONE

THE DREADED "C" WORD

BEFORE WE GET INTO aligning culture and strategy, there are a few things you should know about culture, starting with why I titled this chapter "The Dreaded 'C' Word." Fortunately, the idea that an organization has a culture has been around long enough that it is no longer viewed as just another popular myth or fad perpetuated by consultants looking for a way to make a lot of money. It may seem hard to believe, but it was less than ten years ago that I had a conversation with a senior leader on exactly this topic.

The unfortunate truth is that culture continues to be viewed by many leaders as abstract, vague, and complex. This is understandable given that most definitions use terms such as *values*, *beliefs*, *shared assumptions*, and *behaviors*, which are commonly associated with the fields of psychology and organizational behavior. It isn't a stretch to understand why a lot of leaders take this to mean you need to be a psychologist or have a degree in the behavioral sciences to effectively lead culture change.

The good news is this is not the case. **In fact, leaders build culture every day, although they often don't realize it.** For example, the things they measure and reward send a strong message to employees regarding what is important and valued. To illustrate, let's say a leader believes that efficient and effective processes are critical to success. The leader then identifies metrics to evaluate process performance and sets department and individual goals based on these metrics. In most North American organizations, performance in terms of goals has a significant impact on an employee's rating at year-end appraisals, which in turn determines their compensation and affects their potential for advancement. Can you guess what happens? Barring obstacles such as a lack of skills and knowledge, most employees will adapt their behavior to achieve their goals, which, in this case, could mean consistently following processes, identifying process breakdowns, and implementing process improvements. If this behavior is sustained over time, the leader builds a process-oriented culture within his team, department, and possibly the entire organization, depending on the scope of his responsibilities and influence. So, yes, while culture alignment and change do require that we examine things like beliefs and behaviors, this is not in a vacuum, and we don't start with them. But before we dig into that, let's go over some basics.

WHAT IS ORGANIZATIONAL CULTURE?

Organizational culture encompasses the values, underlying beliefs, and assumptions that guide action and are learned and shared by members of groups as they strive to achieve the organization's goals and fulfill its purpose.

The bedrock of culture is the organization's belief system, which consists of the assumptions, beliefs, and values shared by its members. This belief system provides guidelines and rules for behavior and influences how people perceive, think about, and feel about things. Importantly, it also contains the anxiety of dealing with an unpredictable and uncertain environment. In other words, an organization's culture tells people what is right versus wrong and explains cause and effect, thereby influencing decisions and actions. Over time, this belief system becomes deeply embedded in the way things are done in an organization, shaping its identity and making it unique from every other organization.

Understanding how beliefs influence behavior is critical to our ability to successfully realign and change culture. The reason is simple: if we want to achieve a different outcome, people need to do things differently, which usually requires new and different behavior. However, for behaviors to change, the belief system that is the basis for the behavior—the why we do things this way—must also change. The best way to explain this is with an example.

CULTURE IN ACTION: DECISION-MAKING AT A MOBILE TELECOM SERVICES COMPANY

In 1998, I was conducting doctoral research on culture change in mergers and acquisitions. My research, which lasted a year, focused on the acquisition of a young, fast-growing national US mobile telecom services provider by a large, mature telecom operator, also known as a telco. The first phase of my research focused on understanding the culture of the mobile telecom company—hereafter referred to as MTC—using interviews and observation as my primary data source. It quickly became clear that, although MTC had only existed for five years, it had a distinct culture. Universally, employees at every level used words like *entrepreneurial, innovative, energized,* and *fast-moving* when they spoke with me. I also observed this in action in a number of ways, with one situation in particular standing out.

While interviewing a senior marketing executive—who we will refer to as Mike—he mentioned there was an upcoming meeting that might be beneficial for me to observe. He thought it could provide some insights into the culture and the way decisions were made in the company. His team had been working with an outside advertising agency on a new campaign and was presenting their proposal to the company's executive team at the meeting. His hope was that the executive team would give their approval to move forward with the campaign. This would require that MTC make a significant financial investment, and he wasn't sure which way the decision would go. It also didn't help that he was only able to get one hour on the agenda for his team to present the proposal, answer questions, and leave time for discussion and a decision.

On the day of the meeting, I arrived early to connect with Mike, who introduced me to the MTC advertising campaign team. Noticing the nervous glances between team members, Mike told them that, regardless of the decision, they should feel proud of the work they had done. He encouraged them to believe in what they were doing and presenting and to show the executives they were confident in their belief that the ad campaign was the right solution for the company.

When we entered the meeting room, the executives were standing and talking animatedly with each other. There was such a buzz that I could feel their energy and excitement. At first, I thought it was because they were excited to see the upcoming ad campaign, but I quickly learned that, just that morning, new numbers had been released that showed the company performing well above its new customer acquisition targets and rapidly gaining market share from its competitors. This was great news, as it meant they could depend on a favorable outlook from market analysts that would translate into an uptick in stock price and increase in available capital, enabling them to continue to build out their network and invest in growth.

Once the room quieted and people settled in their seats, Mike dimmed the lights, and a television commercial started to play on a large screen at the front of the room. It was only sixty seconds long, but almost immediately, I could hear a low appreciative rumble and, as I glanced at the faces around the table, see a lot of smiles and nods. The first commercial was followed by two more, and as they played, you could hear the murmur getting louder as the executives began to compare notes. After about ten minutes, the lights came back on, and the chatter amplified, despite Mike's best efforts to regain control of the room. Eventually, the conversations ebbed, and he introduced the marketing director who reported to him—who we will call Susan—and the other members of the ad campaign team.

As Susan stepped to the front of the room, a PowerPoint presentation replaced the television commercial on the screen. Based on the list of topics, she had obviously planned to walk us through the thinking behind the commercials we had just watched, the results of the market research they had conducted, the cost of the campaign, the timing and other considerations, plus other content relevant to a decision of this type and magnitude. She didn't get past the fourth slide.

Approximately ten minutes into her very professional-looking presentation, the CEO raised his hand. He thanked Susan and the ad campaign team for their hard work and said he was certain they had a lot of great information they wanted to share. However, he turned to the other executives and said, "I am sure we can all agree that we are going to move forward with the campaign, so let's get down to business. What do you need from us to make it happen?" End of discussion.

Mike was right. The meeting had provided a great opportunity to see the company's culture in action. After the meeting, I had the chance to circle back with Mike and ask him some questions about what I had observed. The first thing I asked was if this was typical of how decisions were made, to which he replied, "Yes." The executive team, and the leaders who reported to them, relied heavily on their judgment and intuition. They would consider data and analytics if it was clear and concise; however, there had been problems in the past with data integrity, which meant most of the executives, including the CEO, didn't trust it. They were also reluctant to invest the time to gather additional data and complete a comprehensive analysis, believing this had limited value and would slow the company down.

I also asked him about the CEO interrupting the presentation and basically making a unilateral decision on such a significant matter. He smiled as he said he had expected that this would happen. He explained that the CEO was very bright and impatient. When he believed he had enough information, he made a decision. Mike went on to explain that this was an example of how the company valued speed and was willing to take risks. It was what made it entrepreneurial—there was no fear. Later, when I spoke with the CEO, he confirmed what Mike told me. Rather than investing time and resources in data analysis and the preparation of a detailed business case, he trusted his judgment and that of the rest of the executive team. If they got it wrong, he was okay with it. After all, as the CEO explained to me, they weren't going to get it right all the time, but they got it right most of the time. They could not afford to be slow and careful if they were going to achieve the customer acquisition numbers required to be taken seriously by the market and gain access to the capital essential for growth.

Another topic I asked Mike about was how, more generally, meetings were run, as this can often be useful in getting to know a company's culture. Specifically, I was interested in understanding why materials had not been sent out in advance of the ad campaign meeting even though the team was asking for a decision. I was also curious to know if minutes were taken, if agendas were followed, if behavior norms or ground rules were identified and abided, and so on and so forth. Mike's answer was that people at this company were pragmatic. They focused on getting things done as expediently as possible. There was so much happening so quickly that they tended to operate in the here and now. If he sent out materials in advance, they wouldn't get looked at and his team would have wasted time on something that had no value. As far as documenting discussions and decisions made at meetings, this happened if the person leading the meeting felt it was important. For the most part, people were expected to take their own notes and deliver what they agreed to do at the meeting.

Finally, I asked Mike why he had decided to ask Susan, his direct report, to make the presentation to the executive team instead of doing this himself, especially given its importance. He smiled and said he wondered if I would ask about this. At his past company, he would never have done this, as it would have been like throwing a lamb to the wolves. Things were different at MTC. He and most other leaders believed they hired capable, experienced, smart people and needed to trust them to do their jobs. He went on to explain that he made himself available if they wanted his input or advice, but he didn't force his opinion on them, and he most definitely didn't micromanage. Sure, when it was something as big as this, he asked that Susan review the presentation with him early enough that changes could be made before it was shared with the executive team; however, this was the exception.

This is just one example of many that I gathered over the course of this phase of my research. What emerged was a clear picture of a company with an entrepreneurial culture. A company that valued speed, agility, flexibility, responsiveness, adaptability, innovation, risk-taking, and resilience. A company that viewed anything that hinted at bureaucracy as the enemy and a barrier to success.

So, what can we learn from this?

Lesson #1 — Beliefs drive behavior that leads to specific outcomes.

The point of sharing this story is to illustrate how beliefs drive behavior that leads to specific outcomes. In this case, the goal of the mobile telecom company was to aggressively grow its customer base and its share of the very competitive, fast-moving mobile telecommunications market. Their strategy was to offer aggressive pricing options that would undercut those of its competitors. This meant that profit margins would be slim or nonexistent at the onset; however, once the company had established a firm foothold in the market, it would take the necessary steps and adjust its pricing strategy as well as look at other options. To execute their strategy and accomplish their goals, the executive team believed the company needed to have an entrepreneurial culture unencumbered by bureaucracy.

Specifically, they believed the company and its members needed to be fast, flexible, responsive, adaptable, and agile. For this to happen, it was essential they hire self-motivated, bright people who could quickly assess a situation and be depended on to make the right decision most of the time. They also needed leaders who knew how to delegate and empower people while at the same time holding them accountable for results.

They recognized that the company needed to move quickly when an opportunity presented itself. There may be limited data and information available, and they couldn't afford the time required to do an exhaustive analysis. They needed to rely on their own and others' smarts and experience, take risks, and bounce back quickly when they encountered the inevitable bumps in the road.

Once we understand these core beliefs, it is easy to explain the behavior I observed (see table 1 below). The current culture existed because senior leaders believed this was what was needed to execute the company's strategy and achieve its goals. It is worth noting that this culture is specific to MTC and, while we might see similar beliefs in other startups, it is unlikely we will find another company with an identical culture. This is because of differences in context, leadership philosophy and values, and strategy. Not to mention, there are many other dimensions to organizational culture in addition to those identified below.

Beliefs:

- We need to move fast to beat the competition.
- Intuition is more valuable than data—we can't afford analysis paralysis. If we trust our instincts and experience, we will get things right most of the time.
- We need to take risks, experiment, and accept that success comes after failure.
- Bureaucracy is the enemy—it slows us down and gets in the way of forward progress.
- We hire experienced, talented people and need to trust them to do their jobs, not tell them how to do them.

Behaviors and Practices:

- External focus, aggressive—see an opportunity or an opening and go after it.
- Decisive—make decisions quickly, get the minimum amount of data and analysis and decide, and rely on experience.
- Fearless—tolerate uncertainty and ambiguity, take risks, and make mistakes and learn from them.
- Resilient—bounce back quickly from mistakes and failures.
- Noncompliance and process avoidance—allow for lots of exceptions to policies, and tolerate noncompliance to policies and procedures.
- Flexible and adaptable—every day is different, priorities change, and employees rarely do the same thing the same way twice.
- Delegate and empower—use judgment and discretion to make decisions, have the authority to act, and take responsibility for the outcomes.
- Can-do attitude, results-oriented, sense of urgency—do whatever it takes to get results.

Outcomes:

- Rapid growth in new customers and market share.
- Big wins in some key markets, resulting in major gains of new customers.
- Some significant investments that don't achieve the expected returns.
- Innovative customer acquisition strategies.
- High waste and operating costs.
- Inefficient and ineffective processes.

- Redundancies and duplicated effort
- Interesting and challenging work attracts top talent.
- High productivity per employee.
- Below-industry-average employee attrition.
- Above-industry-standards customer satisfaction.

Lesson #2 — Culture reduces people's anxiety and shapes identity.

Culture also reduces people's anxiety. Because there is a predictable and widely accepted way of doing things, people know and understand the unwritten rules and act accordingly, without fear of censure. Not only that, but culture shapes an organization's identity, which, when it aligns with people's personal values, fosters a sense of connection and belonging. When this identity is recognized outside the organization, we usually see people with similar values regarding it as an attractive place to work. Of course, the reverse is also true. If someone believes a company's values are not aligned with their personal values, it is highly likely they will seek employment elsewhere. As more people join the company with these shared values, the culture and identity continue to strengthen and become even more deeply embedded.

Lesson #3 — Culture influences every aspect of organizational life.

Organizational culture is insidious in that it influences every aspect of the organization, not just behavior. This includes its structures and the design of its policies, processes, and systems. You can see an organization's culture in action all around you if you are alert to the signs. For example, whenever I visit a client's site, especially for the first time, I look for cues that provide insights into their culture. This includes things as simple as the design of the lobby. Whereas one company might celebrate its history and accomplishments, another might highlight social responsibility and sustainability. One might be formal and feel very corporate (suits and ties only please), while another might be casual and relaxed (think comfy chairs and cushions). In the case of the mobile telecom company, their lobby was bright and modern and decorated with strategically placed images of customers using the company's products. The message was clear that this was not a typical stodgy telco. This company was new and exciting and, best of all, focused on you, their customer.

CULTURE IN ACTION, PART TWO: THE ACQUISITION OF MTC

The second phase of my research shifted focus to the transition stage after the acquisition deal closed. This phase lasted three months, during which I continued to conduct interviews and observe with the objective of learning what changes, if any, the acquiring company, the telco, would make at their acquisition, MTC, and how this might affect its culture.

Unlike many acquisitions I have been involved in over the years, the telco decided to take its time before making significant changes. Its leaders recognized that the reason MTC had been successful was its entrepreneurial culture. They also recognized that this was in stark contrast to their own more corporate, process-driven culture. Moving too quickly could damage MTC's culture and negatively impact morale, performance, and results, thereby eroding the value of their acquisition. The one exception they made was to replace the mobile telecom company's chief financial officer (CFO) with a senior finance executive from their company. The finance executive—whom we will call Doug—was a long-term telco employee with twenty-five years of experience in the industry. He was a CPA by profession, steadily advancing in his career, as he proved that he could be relied on to run a tight, high-performing finance function. The telco CEO had a suspicion that what he was hearing and seeing from MTC's CEO and other executives was overly positive and failed to paint a complete or accurate picture of the real situation. From experience, he had learned that acquired companies tended to try to show their company in the best light. While understandable, this meant that he needed to do his own investigation to discover the truth. He chose Doug to do this on his behalf, as he was confident that if anyone could separate fact from fiction, Doug was the person to do it.

For the next three months, I spent a great deal of time speaking with and observing Doug and the finance team. Doug used his first thirty days at MTC to gather information and validate what he was learning. He met with each executive several times, attended their meetings, asked a lot of questions, listened, and observed. He also tasked the finance team with providing financial data and analysis. He used this as an opportunity to assess the capability of the people on his team and identify the changes he believed were needed to improve internal processes and systems. In speaking with members of the finance team, it was clear that Doug's leadership style, priorities, and expectations were very different from those of his predecessor. In short, Doug wasn't overtly critical, but the things he asked for and the difficulty the team had delivering them made it clear that changes were coming. This led to a great deal of anxiety and apprehension as the team began to speculate on what this might mean for them personally. Would Doug replace them with people from the telco? Would their jobs and roles change?

Would they have to deal with a lot of bureaucracy?

At the end of his first month, I met with Doug to ask him about his experience and what he had learned about MTC. Doug described the company's entrepreneurial culture, making a point of saying how much he respected and admired what the executive team had achieved. He then shared that before he accepted this assignment, he met with his boss, the telco CEO, and had a frank conversation, during which they shared their perceptions of MTC and its executive team. He told me they had the same concern, which was that, while the company was growing fast, they weren't seeing this translate into profits. The question Doug needed to answer was why.

The answer, Doug believed, was that the executive team had made the decision to prioritize new customer acquisition at any cost. While this made sense at first, he and the telco CEO believed they needed to rethink this and find a way to profitably grow the company. This meant they needed to cut costs, which would require remedying sorely lacking financial and management discipline. When I asked him why he said this, he provided an example of a meeting much like the one I observed regarding the advertising campaign. The objective of the meeting was to decide whether to add more cell towers in one of their regions. This would require a sizable financial investment and, as such, he expected that the operations department would provide him with the business case so he could review it before the meeting. When this didn't happen, he expected that it would be presented at the meeting; however, he was disappointed. While the operations build team provided a cost estimate, the assumptions this was based on were weak, and they failed to estimate the potential return on investment. In other words, operations expected him to support the decision to invest without providing the information he and the rest of the executive team needed. After the meeting, he went immediately to the director of financial planning and analysis, who reported to him, and asked why he allowed this to happen. I watched as the director's face turned white and he almost literally sank into his chair. Doug, to his credit, also noticed this and quickly said he wasn't blaming the director, but he needed to understand why this was happening.

This is where I am going to pause the story and take a moment to talk about what we can learn from what I just shared. If you're wondering what happened next, stay tuned, as the story continues in the next chapter.

Lesson #4 — Culture isn't good or bad; it serves a purpose.

Organizational cultures exist for a reason, which is to serve a specific purpose. Neither the entrepreneurial culture the executive team had built nor the disciplined culture that Doug and the telco CEO preferred was better or worse than the other. Each was appropriate for the company and the situation at the time.

Before the acquisition, MTC was in fast-growth-startup mode and needed to be flexible, adaptable, agile, and opportunistic if it was going to establish a solid foothold in the market. However, after it was acquired, the senior leaders of the larger, mature telco decided that MTC needed to transition from startup to operating mode and turn a profit versus being singularly focused on acquiring new customers. With this change in direction, MTC had to shift its focus to find efficiencies and lower operating costs, which required tighter controls and a more disciplined culture.

It is these types of events that often trigger the need for culture change. In some cases, the event is initiated in response to a significant threat or new opportunity in the external environment. For the company to survive, and hopefully thrive, it must change its strategy or operating model, or both, which requires the company to do things differently than it has in the past. Of course, a change in strategy and operating model can be preemptive and driven internally, as sometimes happens when a company experiences rapid growth or internal innovation or shifts its attention to new markets. Mergers and acquisitions, divestitures, or a change in CEO or executive leadership are also common catalysts for change. However, the extent to which the change effort is successful varies significantly, in part because of the way it is approached (I am going to talk about this in more detail later in this book), which brings us to lesson five.

Lesson #5 — Culture is "sticky."

Culture, and the belief system that is its foundation, is so deeply embedded and effective that it is commonplace to see people engage in rationalization and denial when it is threatened or challenged. Consider for a moment how people who worked at MTC, including the executive team, felt when Doug told them the company needed more financial and management discipline. It was not pretty. They felt a strong connection to the company and to one another because of the values they shared and their belief in the power of an entrepreneurial culture. Furthermore, the company was successful because of this entrepreneurial culture and the talented and dedicated people who had worked to build it. Their initial reaction was disbelief and denial, followed in short order by anger and resentment. Many people even threatened to quit if the culture changed. Others decided to stay quiet and wait it out. This is a classic example of defensive routines and why culture is "sticky"—it is tenacious and difficult to change.

If you have ever been part of an acquisition, you probably have personal experience with these cultural defensive routines in action. Anything the acquiring company does or says that people perceive as different from the way they normally do things can be viewed as a threat and met with resistance. This is one of the main reasons it is estimated that 70–90 percent of mergers and acquisitions and other major change efforts fail to achieve their goals.[4] There are, of course, a few exceptions, such as when an acquiring company comes to the rescue and is viewed as a hero who offers the potential for a brighter future. In this situation, people are dissatisfied with current working conditions and are hoping for a change. The promise of a better future overrides the threat of the unknown and minimizes or eliminates resistance. These cases are, however, not the norm.

These cultural defensive routines are, however, not isolated to mergers and acquisitions. They are triggered by any significant change that requires a different way of working and behaving. For example, the implementation of an enterprise technology solution is typically accompanied by changes in core work processes, roles, and responsibilities that directly affect how employees work and interact. A shift in balance from an emphasis on innovation to an emphasis on cost reduction and operational efficiency or a new strategy that doubles down on differentiating the customer experience will require that people do things differently and behave in new ways. To expect that employees will readily change their behavior and work in different ways is naïve and unrealistic. Yet, there is hope. I am certain you have seen numerous examples of people adapting their behavior to fit in or be effective in new situations.

Think for a moment about new employees entering your organization. They likely have only a superficial knowledge of the inner workings of your company; however, it doesn't take long before they start behaving in the "correct way" to fit in and be accepted. But how do they learn what the "correct way" is? A certain amount is communicated directly by their manager, peers, and perhaps human resources or from an employee handbook, website, or training; however, even more is acquired through observation and direct experience. By simply being a part of the organization and experiencing the way things get done on a day-to-day basis, people learn, often without realizing it, the organization's values, shared assumptions, and beliefs.

Especially influential are the words and actions of people in leadership roles and other positions of power and influence. New and existing employees alike watch these people for signs regarding the right and expected way to behave and moderate their behavior accordingly. If a leader is consistently late for meetings, employees know it is okay if they are also unpunctual. On the other hand, if a new leader joins the company who is always early or on time for meetings, you will soon see employees doing the same. Ultimately, culture is created with shared experience, but it is the leaders who initiate this process by acting out their beliefs, values, and assumptions in the behaviors they demonstrate and the practices they use. The following chapter continues the story of MTC, diving deeper into the role leaders play in shaping and changing culture.

CHAPTER TWO

THE POWER OF
INTENTIONAL LEADERSHIP

EARLIER, I STATED THAT leaders are the single most important factor in determining the success of any culture alignment and change effort. This goes beyond committing time, people, and money to the change effort; it requires being personally involved in a meaningful way. They must lead the way, which means not just telling but showing others what is expected, making tough decisions, and creating the conditions for success. It can't be a nice-to-do item, nor can it be delegated to human resources, other leaders, or outside experts. They must intentionally use the tools available to create a culture aligned with strategy to achieve the organization's goals. In other words, they need to build a culture by design versus allowing the culture to emerge by default. Of course, they are going to need help, as very few leaders have the knowledge, background, and experience required to do this effectively or efficiently. This is where you come in. You can provide the guidance and support they need to be successful.

LEADERSHIP IN ACTION: BUILDING A CULTURE BY DESIGN AT A MOBILE TELECOM SERVICES COMPANY

When we left off in chapter one, Doug had just described a meeting he attended during which a decision was made to build new cell towers at significant cost to the company without knowing the potential return on investment. The decision was made despite his voting against the proposal, and he was not happy. The way he explained it, the meeting showed the company's entrepreneurial culture, its penchant for speed and willingness to accept risk on full display. It also showed, to paraphrase his words, the company's allergic reaction to anything resembling discipline, structure, or process.

With me tagging along to observe, Doug took his frustration out on the director of financial planning and analysis, using very few words to make it clear he was disappointed and expected better. He wasn't in a better mood after the finance director told him that he was not aware of the operations department's plans to build the cell towers. They had not contacted him or anyone on his team to help with the financials or preparation of the business case. He went on to explain that this happened all the time, as most of the executives and their teams didn't trust the financial data or believe they needed assistance.

After the meeting, Doug decided to do some more investigating into the company's capital expenditures. He soon discovered that what the finance director had told him was true. The financial data he was able to gather had glaring gaps, making it almost useless for decision-making and financial management in general. Furthermore, the metrics used to measure the performance of capital projects failed to provide fundamental information on the rate of return, net present value, and payback period. The result was a lack of transparency and accountability, which contributed to poor decision-making and, he suspected, inflated costs. The more questions he asked and the more investigating he did, the more he confirmed his suspicion that discipline in general was simply not part of the culture. He saw examples everywhere he looked, from day-to-day practices such as the way meetings were run to decisions involving millions of dollars. While the entrepreneurial spirit was great, the lack of discipline was costing the company large sums of money due to rework, redundancies, poor decisions, and so on and so forth. The challenge, as he saw it, was to introduce more discipline without crushing innovation and agility.

Although he couldn't do anything about the decision to build the new cell towers, Doug was determined that similar situations would not occur in future. In other words, he made the decision to build a culture by design. He accomplished this by making intentional choices about his words and behavior; the practices he used; the processes and policies he implemented; and the design of roles, responsibilities, and reporting relationships, among many other things. His choices were anchored by his belief in the need for greater discipline, especially in financial management and decision-making. As an aside, when Doug talked about the need for greater discipline, he always included the "why." Why is discipline important? This is simply another way of stating beliefs without explicitly naming them as such.

Fast-forward four months. As part of my research, I arranged to speak with members of the finance team and other executives to learn about their early experience with the post-acquisition transition. In my interviews, I heard story after story about how Doug was single-handedly changing the culture at MTC from, to paraphrase one executive, maybe a bit too loosey-goosey to much more structured and disciplined. Not everyone was a fan, and some even went so far as to accuse him of stifling the company's entrepreneurial spirit; however, they respected him. From the beginning, Doug was clear regarding his intentions and his belief that the company needed more financial and management discipline if it was to thrive and grow. He was consistent with his words and actions. Everyone knew exactly where Doug stood on the subject, and no one questioned that he was doing what he believed was best for the company.

A few months later, when I again spoke with members of the finance team, they shared that, while it was still early, the CEO was disappointed with the results they were seeing from the investment in the new cell towers. The project was experiencing delays and significant cost overruns. Questions were being asked about how the build team was handling the project, including suggestions that they lacked the necessary program and project management skills. This was a shocking change in tone and content from just a few months prior. So, what exactly did Doug do to achieve significant culture change in such a short period of time?

BUILDING A CULTURE BY DESIGN: BEHAVIORS AND PRACTICES

Recognizing the difficulties in attempting to tackle the issue at the enterprise level, Doug decided to focus on things within his immediate control and sphere of influence. He began by introducing practices designed to bring more discipline into the way the finance team worked, starting with meetings and appointments. Doug reinforced these practices with his own behavior. For example, he made it clear that people were expected to be on time and prepared when attending meetings, no exceptions and no excuses.

To schedule an appointment with Doug, people had to explain why the meeting was required and the expected outcome. If his input or a decision was required, relevant background information was to be provided so he could review it prior to the meeting. Appointment times were strictly adhered to. If someone was more than five minutes late, the appointment was automatically canceled, and the person was forced to reschedule. This was a big deal, as it was extremely difficult getting time with him. It could be weeks before the next opening in his schedule. People quickly learned to be on time.

When it came to preparing for meetings, Doug read everything provided in advance. If the work wasn't up to his standards, he would send it back and, in some cases, cancel the appointment. Initially, he provided clear written feedback as to what was missing and questions that needed to be answered. He would do so once. After that, the person was expected to figure out what was missing and fix it.

At the end of one-on-one meetings, he provided feedback including what was done well and what needed to be improved for the next time. For example, he expected people to provide a recommendation with their rationale when asking him for input or a decision. His feedback also included coaching to help the person improve the quality of their recommendations.

Doug was always on time, and he expected the same of others. He made a habit of arriving at least five minutes early for every meeting. His schedule included time for travel to meetings, unexpected requests, preparation, and other unplanned events. While emergencies occasionally required a change to his schedule, these were the exception, and he made sure there was time built in to allow for canceled appointments to be rescheduled at an early date. If the meeting was late starting, he would wait ten minutes, then leave. Initially, this was a problem with his boss and peers; however, he was able to manage the issue by agreeing to return to meetings if required.

The important thing is that he got their attention and made his point.

Consistent with this practice, Doug also started and ended meetings exactly at the scheduled time. If the meeting was to start at 9:00 a.m., he locked the door at 9:10 a.m. and started the meeting regardless of who was or was not in attendance, including his boss and peers. This caused quite a stir at the beginning. You can imagine the look on the CEO's face when he arrived at a meeting to discover the door was locked and he had to wait for a break in the conversation to be allowed to enter the room. He was not amused. As told by another executive, the CEO raised the issue at his next executive team meeting. He reminded Doug that there were situations beyond his control that he sometimes had to deal with, and this caused him to be late; however, he also admitted this was not always the case. In the future, if he was going to be late, his assistant would let Doug know, otherwise he would do his best to arrive on time. This implied that the other executives should do the same.

Doug also introduced practices designed to improve meeting effectiveness. These included publishing the meeting agenda, with background information, for review one week ahead of the meeting date. The agenda included the "ask" for each item, such as "provide input," "identify issues or obstacles," "make a decision," or "provide information." Items that fell into the "provide information" category were reviewed to determine if they could be effectively addressed in other ways and removed from the agenda. The amount of time allowed for each agenda item was determined by the complexity of the topic and the ask. In the meeting, these timelines were strictly adhered to, albeit with some growing pains at the outset. Initially, agenda items were closed without having achieved the ask. As the team got better at using the available time, this became the exception rather than the rule.

Doug also implemented meeting principles that clearly defined expectations for behavior. These were posted on the meeting room wall and used as a form of performance review at the end of each meeting. Specifically, the team used a "green, yellow, red" scorecard for each principle to indicate what they did well and what they needed to do better. A brief discussion of the "do better" principles clarified expected changes for the next meeting. These included being present and engaged, which meant turning off cell phones and other nonessential devices. To address potential emergencies, he provided a contact person outside the meeting. Early on in his tenure, someone attending one of Doug's meetings made the mistake of not taking him seriously and answered a call. Doug stopped the discussion, walked up to the person, and held out his hand for the phone. He told the person at the other end to call back when the meeting was over and turned off the phone. He then took the phone and dropped it in the garbage can. Everyone laughed, and the discussion continued. At the break, the phone's owner approached Doug and apologized, asking if he could have his phone back. Doug said no. The rules were clear, and there needed to be consequences. If he wanted a phone, he was going to have to get a new one. The story traveled through the building like wildfire. Doug returned the phone later that day, but he had made his point.

Within days, people began to show up on time for their appointments and meetings with Doug. Within a few weeks, people consistently arrived on time for all meetings, not just Doug's meetings but also those hosted by others. Meetings became more efficient and effective, and people appreciated that they could depend on the fact that they would always end on time.

This discipline wasn't restricted to appointments and meetings. Doug applied the same principles to performance management, written communication, business case preparation, and an assortment of other practices. He used every opportunity to bring greater discipline into day-to-day work and interactions (see table 2 below). Four months later, members of the finance team described a significant, observable culture shift toward greater discipline. Although initially limited to the finance team, they saw evidence of change in other leaders and teams due to the scope of Doug's influence. Contrary to most popular views, this is an example of how culture change can happen in months, not years, as most experts believe.[5]

Beliefs:
- To be sustainable, we need to make money. To make money, we need to manage our costs. To manage our costs, we need good data. To make good decisions, we need to use the right data effectively.
- Discipline increases efficiency and effectiveness and lowers costs, making us more profitable.
- Compliance with clear policies, procedures, and processes ensures we consistently achieve the right outcomes.

Behaviors and Practices:
- Decision-making—business cases prepared for large financial investment; decisions based on data and analytics.
- Controls—delegation of authority for financial and hiring decisions lowered; expense guidelines followed for travel and living.

- Meeting management—meetings start and end on time, with agenda, objectives, and materials sent in advance.
- Management discipline— project management discipline is implemented for all major projects.
- Accountability—managers asked to explain all deviations from financial budgets and plans.

Outcomes:
- Financial investments achieve expected results.
- Less waste due to poor decisions; improved performance of growth initiatives.
- Employee productivity and engagement decrease.
- Meeting efficiency and effectiveness improve.
- Travel and living expenses at or below target.
- Fiscal restraint practiced; actual results come in at budget.
- Major projects completed on time and within budget.
- Lower waste and decreased operating costs.

What can we learn from this?

Lesson #6—Leaders can increase the effectiveness of their change efforts using their sphere of influence.
Doug intentionally chose to initially focus his change effort primarily on the finance function because it reported to him and it was where he had the greatest power to influence change. It was at the core of his sphere of influence.[6] A leader's sphere of influence refers to the people and things (policies, processes, structures, spaces, and so on) directly or indirectly affected by his or her actions. The sphere of influence has three elements: the sphere of control, the sphere of influence, and the sphere

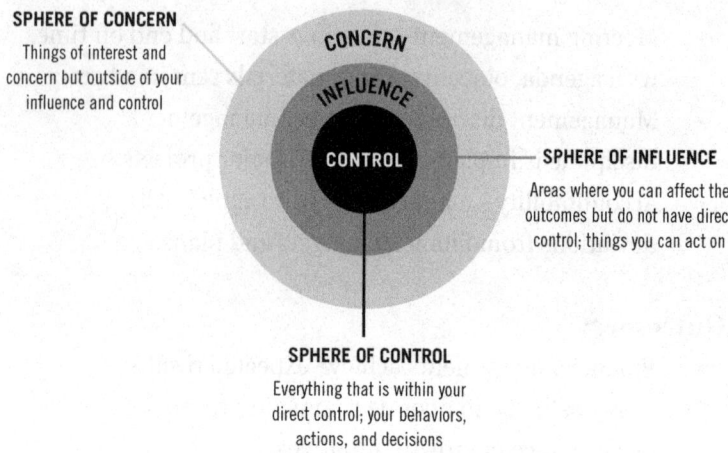

SPHERE OF CONCERN

Things of interest and concern but outside of your influence and control

CONCERN

INFLUENCE

CONTROL

SPHERE OF INFLUENCE

Areas where you can affect the outcomes but do not have direct control; things you can act on

SPHERE OF CONTROL

Everything that is within your direct control; your behaviors, actions, and decisions

Diagram 2: Spheres of influence

of concern.[7] Those things that are directly within a leader's control, such as their behaviors, actions, and decisions, are referred to as their sphere of control. Things that the leader doesn't have direct control over but which they can affect the outcomes of fall within their sphere of influence. An example of this is a CEO who needs to influence the company's board of directors. Finally, those things that are outside the leader's sphere of control and influence but are of interest or concern are referred to as their sphere of concern. These are the things that can cause anxiety due to the feeling of helplessness they create. For example, a CEO is typically very concerned about the company's competitors yet has no control over their actions or decisions. The size and scope of the sphere of influence are determined, in part, by the person's role, responsibilities, and relationships. In other words, the more senior you are, the greater your potential influence and capacity to effect change.

In a small organization, the senior leaders or leadership team is typically involved in most, if not all, aspects of operations. Thus, their sphere of influence is extensive and powerful.

This is what is meant by the phrase, "Their fingerprints are on pretty much everything." Other leaders have influence over some people and things, but this is limited. As an organization grows, we can see an increase in the scope of influence below the senior management level. This does not mean the senior leaders' spheres of influence have diminished. The increase in size and complexity that accompanies growth requires that senior leaders shift more and more of their attention to strategic matters and delegate responsibility for running the business to people at lower levels. As a result, frontline employees, their managers, and their managers' managers may have limited contact or interaction, if any, with senior leaders. The result is an increase in the influence of midlevel managers and the immediate manager. People in these roles directly influence the work experience of the people who report to them and the way things are done within their area of responsibility. They also indirectly affect people and work in adjacent areas. To make matters more complex, leaders can also be found in nonmanagement roles, usually by virtue of their expertise, personality,

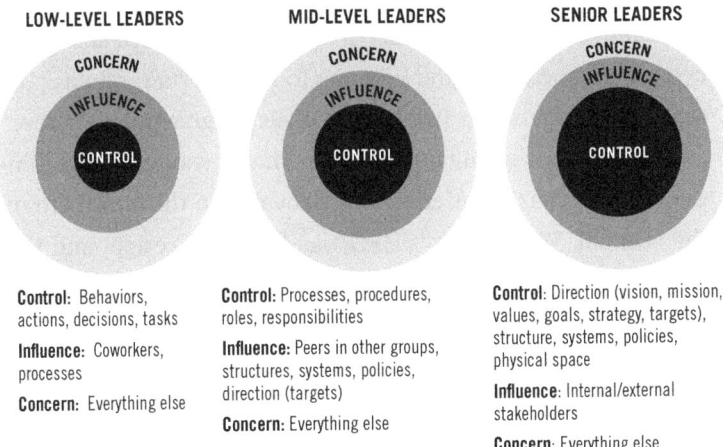

LOW-LEVEL LEADERS   MID-LEVEL LEADERS   SENIOR LEADERS

Control: Behaviors, actions, decisions, tasks

Influence: Coworkers, processes

Concern: Everything else

Control: Processes, procedures, roles, responsibilities

Influence: Peers in other groups, structures, systems, policies, direction (targets)

Concern: Everything else

Control: Direction (vision, mission, values, goals, strategy, targets), structure, systems, policies, physical space

Influence: Internal/external stakeholders

Concern: Everything else

Diagram 3: A leader's sphere of influence

or credibility. The result is a complex web of shared connections and work, creating overlapping spheres of influence.

In sum, it isn't just people in senior leadership roles who have influence. Anyone in a management position has the capacity to affect the people reporting to them, while highly regarded individuals in nonmanagement roles influence their peers and others in their network. In other words, every leader, regardless of level, can influence culture; however, the extent depends on their sphere of influence.

Lesson #7—Leaders' actions send messages to others.
One of the ways leaders build culture is through their words and, more importantly, their actions. These are like messages that provide people with cues as to the expected way of doing things. When words and actions are consistent—when leaders walk the talk—the message is clear and pretty much guaranteed to influence others to act in a similar manner. This explains why we sometimes see good people do bad things, as in the case of the Wells Fargo financial scandal.

As reported by Forbes, "Wells Fargo executives pressured rank-and-file bank personnel to aggressively cross-sell products to enhance sales and revenue to meet certain quotas. Deception reared its ugly head when Wells Fargo employees then created millions of savings and checking accounts for customers without their knowledge or approval."[8] In the aftermath of the scandal, Wells Fargo's CFO was forced to resign, and the company agreed to pay three billion USD to the US Department of Justice (DOJ) and the Securities and Exchange Commission (SEC) to settle the lawsuit. Unlike Enron and other companies found guilty of fraudulent and unethical actions, Wells Fargo survived, but its credibility was damaged. This case provides an extreme example of the power leaders have to influence others' behavior; however, more often, this happens in less overt ways. Employees notice absolutely everything a leader says and does. If a leader consistently arrives early for a meeting, the leader's direct reports will also arrive early. If the leader always wears the appropriate safety gear on a worksite, people know this is important, and they can expect to be censured if they don't do the same. Of course, the opposite is also true. A leader who is frequently late for meetings and appointments sends the message that it is okay for others to be unpunctual. Likewise, a leader who blames others for their mistakes is implicitly telling people through actions that avoidance of responsibility is okay.

Doug was very aware of this and the importance of sending a clear, consistent message through his words and actions. Being disciplined was easy for him, as this was ingrained in the beliefs that drove his behavior. However, while Doug was careful to be consistent, there were times when people made assumptions based on something he did that appeared to conflict with what he was saying. For example, although Doug said he valued the company's entrepreneurial spirit, he introduced policies that reduced managers' authority to hire new employees and approve expenditures. This was interpreted by many as a shift toward bureaucracy. The reality was that Doug did not view entrepreneurialism and discipline as mutually exclusive. He believed there were aspects of MTC's entrepreneurial culture that needed to be protected, as these had proven invaluable in helping to drive growth. This included its innovative approaches to new customer acquisition; the decisiveness of its leaders; and its laser-like focus on the market, customers, and competitors. However, the company also needed to be profitable, which meant lowering costs and making better capital investment decisions. The problem was that this had never been explained in a way that resonated with employees. As far as Doug was concerned, this should have been obvious, and therefore, no explanation was needed. As a result, employees were left to interpret Doug's words and actions in the context of their personal beliefs.

Lesson #8 — Cultural coherence is only possible when there is 100 percent consistency in words and actions. What happens when there is a perceived disconnect between a leader's words and actions? Answer: people will default to actions as the real message. When Doug reduced managers' decision authority, his actions were interpreted as he—and, by default, the rest of the executive team—no longer trusted managers to make decisions. To these managers, who thrived in an entrepreneurial setting, trust was essential. If this was missing, they believed the company was on track to become slow and bureaucratic like the telco that had acquired them. This was not at all what Doug intended, and it took a great deal of effort to address the issues this created for employee morale and productivity.

Another example of a disconnect in Doug's messaging was candor. Doug told his team that candor was important and he wanted people to openly voice their concerns and let him know the bad news as well as the good news. The problem was that Doug tended to react negatively when he heard bad news or thought someone's idea or thinking was flawed. It only took a few situations like this before his team figured out the rules— how to make Doug believe they were speaking candidly while protecting themselves from harm. Doug was happy thinking employees were being open, honest, and straightforward when the reality was far different—at least until he discovered the truth. To make matters worse, the team learned to view everything Doug said with skepticism. His credibility was damaged, and it would take him a long time to regain it.

In fairness, Doug did a lot more things right than wrong; however, even good leaders make mistakes, which is why they need help. In Doug's case, he misjudged how managers would react and was unaware his behavior would trigger a lack of candor. This could have been avoided, or at least addressed, if Doug had a trusted advisor to make him aware of the impact of his actions on others; however, this was not the case. I could not be his advisor, as doing so would have compromised the credibility of my research, which was not something I was willing to do. Ideally, an HR or OD professional like yourself would have stepped into this role; however, MTC had yet to establish an HR function in-house and instead outsourced this to a third party. The bottom line is that a leader's words and actions must be consistent and model what is expected—no exceptions and no excuses!

Lesson #9—Leaders reinforce culture in day-to-day practices.

In addition to behaviors, Doug also intentionally used day-to-day practices to build discipline into the company's culture. Practices are the repeat patterns of activity or routines that people employ as they go about their work.[9] They are different from processes, which involve the transformation of an input into an output. Practices cover a wide range of routines, including the way decisions are made, information is shared, and people are recognized, just to name a few. They are the building blocks that help to determine "the way things are done around here."

While every employee uses practices to some extent, leaders employ more of them more extensively, which gives them greater influence over culture. This includes the approach they take to developing plans, conducting meetings, managing performance, developing employees, and so on and so forth. To illustrate the effect practices have on culture, contrast meetings that are managed in a structured and disciplined manner with ones that are ad hoc and loosely organized.

Doug employed a very disciplined approach to meetings, assessing their effectiveness by the decisions made, issues resolved, and actions identified. As far as Doug was concerned, relationship building was secondary to achieving these objectives. For example, a carefully designed agenda was sent out well in advance of meetings, along with briefing notes and reports with clear instructions regarding expected action, such as "read this prior to the session" and "come prepared with questions." There was also a clear ask, such as "this item requires a decision" or "so-and-so seeks feedback." Meetings started on time, and the agenda was tightly managed. The rules of engagement were clear and closely monitored. Minutes were taken, with decisions and actions noted and distributed to the attendees.

In contrast, loosely organized meetings are very different. If there is an agenda, it may or may not be followed. It might be sent out in advance and include some premeeting materials, but there is an implicit understanding that this is a guideline rather than a commitment. Often, a good portion of the agenda is never reached, and this is okay. Similarly, there may or may not be minutes, depending on what happens in the meeting and if any decisions are made or actions identified.

Lesson #10—Intentionally using a network of practices can accelerate culture change.

If the leader uses multiple practices based on the same set of beliefs, there is a compounding and reinforcing effect. For instance, a leader who believes relationships are critical might build time for this into meetings and take a consultative and inclusive approach to decision-making and problem-solving. Similarly, a leader like Doug who believes discipline and efficiency are the keys to success may apply other practices, such as setting clear objectives and systematically monitoring and measuring performance. The more practices a leader uses, the more impact they have on culture. This is what I refer to as the intentional use of a network of practices to accelerate culture change.

One more thing to note about practices: the practices used by leaders not only reflect their beliefs but are indicators of their expectations of others. If a leader believes discipline is important, he will assess others' performance and abilities using this as a criterion. Anyone who demonstrates a lack of discipline, as perceived by the leader, risks being judged negatively. In fact, practices may be even more influential than behavior, as they directly affect the way people work and interact and how they are perceived by others.

BUILDING A CULTURE BY DESIGN: CREATING THE CONDITIONS FOR SUSTAINED SUCCESS

Doug's primary goal was to increase the discipline applied to cost management and decision-making by implementing initiatives that would, to paraphrase the words of one employee, encourage deeper economic and operational analysis from both a tool and process perspective. The behaviors and practices he introduced were only the beginning. Doug recognized that addressing the big issues at the enterprise level required a substantial investment in core processes and technology, as well as changes to the way the finance department was structured. These changes required careful planning and project management and were implemented over a period of twenty-four months.

The phasing of these changes was important. Doug and the MTC executive team were expected to deliver improved results quickly. The telco was not going to wait two years for this to happen. The first change he tackled was the structure of roles and reporting relationships in the finance function. Prior to Doug taking over as CFO, most members of the finance team were generalists who reported directly to business unit leaders. Their responsibilities were broad and included budgeting, cost and sales estimates, expense management, reporting, and anything else the business unit leader needed. A few specialists reported directly to the CFO and handled corporate fiduciary requirements, such as treasury, investor relations, financial planning and analysis (FP&A), and accounting.

Given their reporting relationship, the finance generalists did what was expected and concentrated their efforts on meeting the needs of the business unit leaders. After all, it was the business unit leaders who rated their performance at year-end, and this directly affected their compensation. However, as a result, every business unit did things differently. They each had their own way of estimating sales and revenue, budgeting, reporting, managing costs, analyzing results, and so on. When it came time to pull together financial information at the enterprise level, the corporate team had a mess on their hands, if they could get the information they needed from the business units at all. This led to long delays and inaccurate and incomplete financial information that no one trusted.

The good news was that many of the processes required to solve this problem were already in place. The issue was they were not being followed. One option was to mandate that the business units comply with the corporate finance processes; however, this would put the finance generalists in the difficult position of having to push back on leaders and not deliver what they wanted. This wasn't realistic, given business leaders set the finance generalists' objectives; assessed their performance; determined rewards, including merit increases; and had a significant say in advancement and development opportunities. Asking the generalists to put corporate needs ahead of the business unit and go against the wishes of the business unit leader was setting them up to fail.

In the short term, Doug decided to do things that didn't totally resolve the situation but certainly improved it. The first was to insist that he had a greater role in setting expectations and evaluating the performance of the finance generalists. By making this a shared responsibility, he was able to align their objectives with his priorities while at the same time providing an incentive to consider corporate finance requirements when they prioritized tasks. Second, he sought for the business unit leaders to agree to comply with the processes most critical to addressing the issues with the timeliness and accuracy of financial information. Given the severity and visibility of the problem, it was relatively easy to get the support he needed. With this in place, he quickly deployed resources to ensure expectations were clear and the processes and tools were understood.

With the immediate problem addressed, Doug, with input from his finance team, directed his attention to making the changes required to achieve his goal of increasing the discipline applied to cost management and decision-making. To this end, he identified and set about implementing a set of initiatives targeted at improving the timeliness, quality, and quantity of financial information available to business unit leaders. This included launching a major activity-based costing (ABC) initiative, adding rigor to the approval process for new hires and capital funding, and spearheading a new business priority and objective-setting process. He also partnered with the company's chief information officer (CIO) to lead the implementation of a decision support system (data and analytics). These initiatives were prioritized and carefully planned so as not to disrupt business as usual while ensuring progress was made as quickly as possible. Recognizing this was not a strength in finance or elsewhere, Doug also established and staffed a new project management office (PMO). The PMO was responsible for helping the various project teams effectively plan, implement, monitor, and report on their progress. Although not entirely successful, due to new hires who clashed with the existing culture, it resulted in a level of consistency and transparency that had been absent in past initiatives.

Approximately six months after the business leaders agreed to follow the prioritized finance processes, there continued to be major issues with the timeliness and accuracy of financial information. Despite their assurances, the business leaders had quickly reverted to their old ways of doing things, insisting that the finance generalists make their needs a priority. While most of the generalists did their best to deliver the information required by corporate, workload pressures and competing demands meant that delays and inaccurate and incomplete information were common. The situation came to a head when the company was called to task by outside analysts for overestimating projected revenue and failing to notify the market that financial targets were going to be missed. Although painful, this was the opening Doug needed to restructure the finance function. He immediately moved to change reporting relationships so the generalists reported directly to him and indirectly to the business unit leaders. Making this happen was not easy. The business unit leaders fought hard to maintain the status quo. They argued that the current structure allowed them to focus their finance staff on business priorities, such as pricing, preparing competitive bids, and so on. They feared that a centralized structure meant they would lose control of these resources, which would cause delays in getting the financial support required to effectively manage their business. In the end, the financial forecasting and reporting issues outweighed their concerns, and the CEO supported Doug's restructuring plan.

Almost overnight, things started to improve. The finance generalists still had a difficult task, as saying no to business unit leaders is never easy. Knowing their boss, Doug, supported them and would step in to help went a long way toward giving them the confidence and courage they needed. Indeed, in the early days, there were many stories of Doug confronting business unit leaders and other C-suite executives who tested the new way of doing things and how, on a few particularly contentious issues, the CEO got involved and made it clear that Doug had his full support. Without this, it was unlikely the change effort would have succeeded. The CEO only had to intervene a few times for the situation to improve, but the message was clear: this was the new world order.

Of course, sustaining the change ultimately depended on finance's ability to deliver timely, accurate financial information that addressed the company's fiduciary obligations and the need for greater discipline in cost management and decision-making.

If the problems had persisted after the change, things would have quickly reverted to the old way of doing things. Fortunately, the changes resulted in an immediate improvement and only got better as the more complex, longer-term initiatives were implemented. Two years after he joined MTC, Doug had achieved his goal of increasing discipline in cost management and decision-making. He also changed the culture.

What can we learn from this?

Lesson #11—Leaders create the conditions for success (environment).

Leaders create the conditions for success by intentionally designing structures, processes, policies, and other elements of the organization to reinforce the desired behaviors and practices. They decide how space is used, what artifacts are on display (or allowed), and what traditions and rituals are practiced. Through the choices they make, leaders create the conditions that encourage and reinforce expected behaviors and practices.

My favorite way to explain this is to use a metaphor of someone trying to lose weight. It is easy to identify the behaviors to start and stop, such as eating more fruits and vegetables, cutting out foods with high levels of sodium and sugar, and exercising more. It's also easy to identify practices to reinforce these behaviors, such as using a phone app to track food consumption and exercise, weighing in on a weekly basis, and attending regular meetings with people who have similar goals. If I do these things, chances are pretty good I am going to lose weight, at least in the short term. The challenge, as many of us know, is overcoming temptation, especially when you're stressed or tired. This is where the environment plays an important role by creating the conditions for success. If the kitchen cupboards are stocked with salty snacks, cookies, and chocolate, eventually, the temptation is going to be too great to resist. Similarly, if other family members are munching away on high-calorie foods and drinks that you love, you're most likely going to cave. Likewise, if you hate going to the gym but make it your main source of exercise, there is no way you will be able to sustain the motivation to keep going. This is what I mean by the environment needing to support the desired behaviors by creating the conditions for success.

We see this same pattern repeated over and over in organizations. A tremendous amount of effort and resources is invested in articulating and communicating the case for change, the importance of living the company's values, and the way employees are expected to behave. These behaviors are then embedded in competency models and various human resource processes, such as talent acquisition, performance management, and so on. There may even be a commitment made to coach and hold leaders accountable for modeling these behaviors. Yet, time and time again, these efforts fail to result in meaningful, sustained behavior and culture change. Why does this happen?

When we ask people to change their behavior but don't align the system to support these behaviors, we are setting them up to fail. Human resource policies, programs, and processes are a critical part of this system. Aligning these to support the desired change is essential and usually happens; however, in many cases, other important parts of the system are ignored. Take legal, for example. In large, mature organizations, the legal team's responsibilities typically include the review and approval of contracts with third parties. In these organizations, it is not unusual to hear stories of long delays and the need for multiple levels of approval to get something done. This often happens for very good reasons, such as the need to protect the organization's best interests, meet its regulatory and legislated obligations, and get the best possible deal with suppliers. It does, however, also contribute to slow decision-making and missed opportunities.

Now, let's say things change. New competitors, emerging technology, and changing market and customer expectations require increased speed and responsiveness to compete. In other words, the organization needs to be more agile, which means decisions must be made swiftly, often with limited information, meaning risks are going to be taken and mistakes made. This is a significant culture change for an organization that has been successful operating in a slow, cautious, and methodical manner. The thing is, for the organization to become agile, the role of legal and many of its core processes and policies need to change. This is threatening not only to legal as a function but to its individual members. It also challenges existing beliefs as to the best and right way of doing things, which triggers defensive routines that result in resistance.

Clear communication of the case for change accompanied by effective implementation of change management practices can help to overcome this resistance to some extent. However, for the change effort to be successful and accomplished in a reasonable time, senior leaders must be actively involved in identifying and implementing the required changes to structures, processes, policies, and so on. To be clear, they are not doing this alone. They need to engage subject matter experts and others whose expertise is critical to arriving at the best possible solution. A leader's role is to challenge, push, and test to ensure changes deliver the expected results. Ultimately, leaders must create the right environment so new behaviors can take root and flourish. They must be willing to make tough, unpopular decisions and hold people accountable to create the conditions for successful culture change.

In this way, we can see the culture begin to shift, sometimes in a matter of months. When senior leaders intentionally use a combination of behaviors and practices and create the conditions for success, amazing things can happen. This is precisely what happened because of Doug's intentional leadership of culture change at the mobile telecom company.

REFLECTING ON DOUG'S STORY

Doug's story is an example of leader-led culture change. He concentrated his efforts on changes within the scope of his role and decision-making authority and used the tools at his immediate disposal to move things forward. This was not a ground-up effort, where employees were engaged in an effort to get their buy-in and support for the change. You may also have noticed that Doug's story doesn't make mention of defining expected behaviors, communicating these to employees, and embedding them in HR processes and practices. Nope, this was an influential leader leading the way through his actions.

That is not to say there isn't value in engaging employees, clearly articulating expected behavior, or aligning HR processes. In fact, these can help to accelerate culture change, as you will see in a later chapter. That said, as noted previously, MTC had outsourced its HR requirements to a third party, which meant the company lacked the internal capability to support the change effort. Furthermore, the third-party organization was contracted to provide basic services and would have needed guidance and direction from MTC. There are, of course, other options, such as hiring consultants; however, this can be costly and time-consuming. Given the circumstances, it is easy to understand why Doug chose not to go this route.

Achieving meaningful and sustained culture change requires that leaders lead the way. They do this by intentionally modeling values and behaviors, using day-to-day practices, and creating the conditions for success. When this is done effectively, culture change is pretty much guaranteed. Even more exciting is the fact that this is something any leader at any level can do. You don't have to be in a senior management position. Anyone in a leadership role can use their words and actions in an intentional and purposeful way to shape and change culture. They may not have the power to change enterprise-level structures and processes, but they can change the culture within their team, and perhaps in doing so, influence the culture of the organization. Furthermore, when a critical mass of leaders purposefully and authentically uses a similar set of behaviors and practices, the potential for positive change increases dramatically. When the organization system is aligned to support the change, well, the sky is the limit.

CHAPTER THREE
CULTURE CHANGE FACTS VERSUS FICTION

FORMAL CULTURE CHANGE INITIATIVES have been around for decades, and yet very few, in my experience, ever achieve their goals. These are the initiatives that are designed specifically for the purpose of understanding and changing culture. The ones that result from someone in a leadership role asking, "Do we have the culture we need to fulfill our mission and achieve our vision?" Or perhaps, "How does our culture compare to our competitors'?" Whatever the question, it triggers the need for information and action, which is, in most cases, delegated to the HR function. There are, of course, some exceptions, as I noted in the story of the mobile telecom services company MTC. However, in this case, I would argue that culture change was the outcome, not the objective of Doug's efforts. His objective was to lower costs and increase profitability, and to do this, he introduced more financial and management discipline into the company, which eventually resulted in culture change.

Personally, I have been involved in dozens of these efforts, learning what works and what doesn't and using this to evolve the way I think about and approach culture change. In this chapter, I share some of the more important lessons I learned in hopes that they will help you make informed choices about how you approach culture change in your organization. To accomplish this, I share the story of a manufacturing company—hereafter referred to as POM—and its efforts to build a more process-oriented culture.

The story and lessons learned from POM unfold in three parts. Part one focuses on understanding the current culture and the actions taken to prepare for the introduction of Lean Six Sigma at the company. This includes a discussion of the role of culture assessments and the difference between culture and climate. Part two continues POM's story eighteen months into the Lean Six Sigma implementation and explores some of the challenges experienced because of the existing culture. This reveals insights into the role of communication and change management and the effectiveness of behavioral approaches to culture change and grassroots change efforts. Part three concludes POM's story by describing how the barriers created by the existing culture were overcome.

CHANGING CULTURE, PART ONE: IMPLEMENTING LEAN SIX SIGMA AT A MANUFACTURING COMPANY

A few years back, I had the opportunity to work with POM's leadership team. The company was founded in the 1970s and continues to be operated by the founding family, whose members hold several of its senior leadership positions. It was, and continues to be, a profitable company, although growth had slowed considerably during the five years before I worked with them. To maintain profit margins, the company aggressively managed costs, slashing expense budgets, negotiating better supply agreements, and eventually even laying off employees for the first time in its history. As part of these efforts, the leadership team also made the decision to invest in a Six Sigma and Lean manufacturing system (Lean Six Sigma) to reduce waste, increase operational efficiency, and improve quality.

The company's senior leadership team recognized that the transition to Lean Six Sigma required expert knowledge and capabilities the company didn't have at the time. This led to the decision to hire a new vice president (VP)—whom we will refer to as Tom—with the required skills and experience to lead the initiative. Tom reported to the chief operating officer (COO), who approved the hiring of a small team to assist him. Tom was also provided with a budget of five million dollars, which some senior leaders felt was excessive, with the expectation the company would start to see a return on its investment within two years.

Given the size of the investment and expectations regarding return, gathering baseline data was critical to Tom's ability to provide evidence that the initiative was achieving the expected results. Tom also realized that the company's culture could be an important factor in determining success. With this in mind, he reached out to the vice president of human resources (VP HR)—whom we will call Diane—and asked for her assistance. Diane decided the first place to start was to conduct a culture assessment of the current culture. The process she chose, with input from Tom, was a culture survey that was sent to the company's employees. The survey she selected was one I designed and have used in organizations across a wide range of industries, sectors, and geographies. Diane believed that using a survey to measure culture before the initiative was launched would help to identify potential challenges they needed to address. She also saw the value of remeasuring the culture after implementation to determine if the culture had changed and identify where further work was needed. Diane selected my culture survey because she saw that it was unique from others of its kind in that, by interpreting the results in context, it provides powerful insights into a company's values and belief system.[10] By contrast, other culture surveys tend to be descriptive and focus on the gaps that exist between a company's culture and industry benchmarks.

Tom was especially interested in what could be learned from the results of the culture dimension that examines process management discipline. This dimension assesses the degree of clarity of core processes, the extent to which there is consistency in implementing core processes, and the effectiveness of continuous process improvement practices. Also of particular interest were the culture dimensions that examined critical success factors such as the clarity of the company's goals and strategy, the effectiveness and openness of communication, and the level of teamwork and collaboration within and between groups. To no one's surprise, the culture survey results confirmed that process discipline was not a strength, nor was compliance with company policies and procedures. What was surprising was the finding that discipline was lacking in other areas, including decision-making and planning. Furthermore, collaboration between teams, especially across functions, was even weaker than expected, as was communication. There were other challenges as well, including candor, which indicated employees did not feel safe to speak up when they had ideas or concerns. Also, while leaders had expected to see high scores on results orientation reflecting employees' can-do mindset, this was not the case.

There was, however, some positive news. The caring, people-oriented culture that senior leaders were so proud of shone through in the survey results. This was a company where every employee was treated as a person and not just someone hired to do a job. According to employees, this was very special and made the company unique in the industry. This is also what had attracted them to work at POM and the main reason they chose to stay even though many believed they could make more money elsewhere. They especially appreciated the company's friendly, supportive, welcoming, inclusive culture and the feeling that they were part of a family where they were appreciated, valued, and respected.

POM Culture Scorecard

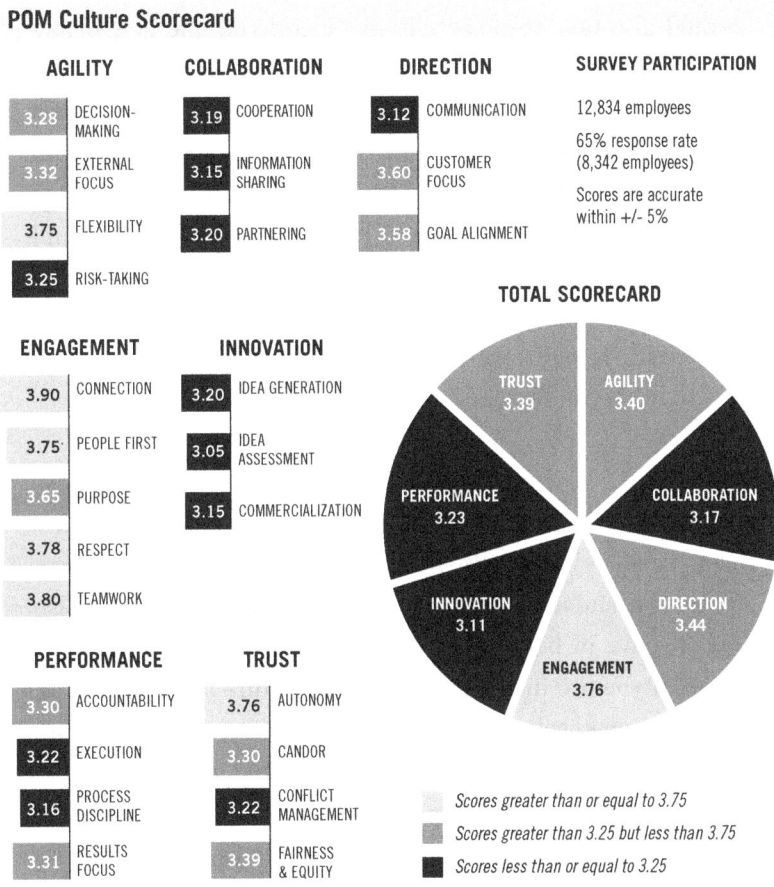

Diagram 4: Manufacturing company culture assessment results summary [11]

These attributes contributed to strong results in employee engagement. Employees were proud of the company and what they had achieved together. They were dedicated; loyal; and, given the chance, were happy to do whatever they could to help the company achieve its goals. Based on these findings, Diane advised Tom that it would be very important to communicate and engage employees during every step of the Lean Six Sigma initiative. Her team would help by supporting this effort. She would also take responsibility for identifying the new behaviors expected of managers and employees in a Lean Six Sigma culture and embedding these in the company's hiring and performance management processes. In addition, her team would support Tom with the design and implementation of a change management strategy. This was a significant commitment and an excellent example of how HR, acting as a strategic business partner, can help to achieve culture change while ensuring ownership remains with the business leader.

So, what can we learn from this?

Lesson #12 — Culture assessments can be helpful but should be used with care.

Culture surveys and other assessments, if well-designed, can provide useful insights into a company's culture. They can also be effective in helping to monitor and measure change over time. If you are interested in using a culture survey, I strongly recommend selecting one that has been designed by culture experts and rigorously tested to ensure the validity and reliability of the results. While there are lots of options available for purchase, many that advertise themselves as culture surveys actually measure organizational climate, employee satisfaction, or employee engagement. For this reason, it is important to do your homework. Otherwise, you risk making decisions based on flawed information.

Another problem occurs when the people interpreting the assessment results and deciding on actions to be taken approach this the wrong way. Most business professionals are trained early in their careers to use tools such as surveys to help identify gaps so they can quickly move into solution mode. They trust that the information they are working with is well-grounded and accurate. Culture surveys are no different, especially when they include external industry benchmarks. In fact, the inclusion of benchmarks can be especially seductive, as they encourage us to focus on the largest gaps between our culture and those of our competitors. While this can be helpful, it is important to consider the organization's context, such as its history, values, leadership philosophy, and strategy. For example, POM is an old family-owned and -operated business. Its culture is a direct reflection of the family's values and their beliefs regarding the best way to run the company. This includes a belief in the power of individuals and teams to achieve the results the company needs to thrive, so this is where they focused their attention and energy. If we were to compare POM's survey results to other manufacturing companies, it is likely we would see some significant gaps, especially in areas related to operational excellence, such as execution and process discipline.

If we didn't understand the family values and beliefs, we might assume the gaps were the result of a lack of management capability, especially when we combined this with the low scores on communication, goal clarity, and collaboration. Based on this, we might reasonably have decided that the company needed to replace some of the managers with better-trained, more experienced people. However, this would have triggered a backlash from employees and damaged the very qualities that differentiated the company from its competitors. It was the company's focus on employee well-being and its high-engagement culture that allowed it to attract and hire top talent in a very competitive marketplace. This is where it can be helpful to engage a culture expert who can help you to understand the assessment results, how the culture is supporting or impeding strategy execution and goal achievement, and what actions to take.

Lesson #13 — Organizational climate and culture are very different.

I mentioned above that many supposed culture surveys actually measure organizational climate, not culture. As you know, organizational culture refers to shared values, beliefs, and assumptions. This belief system is what drives behavior and decisions and determines the way things get done in an organization. On the other hand, organizational climate refers to people's experiences with the culture, including what it is like to work at the company and how they feel about this experience. While culture tends to be stable until beliefs change, climate can vary frequently in response to new events.

For example, POM's leaders genuinely believed that people were critical to the success of the business, which was evident in the time they spent getting to know individual employees, the investment they made in employee training and development, and the policies they put in place to support employee well-being. When the company experienced financial challenges, leaders were forced to make the difficult decision to lay off some employees. If we had conducted the survey immediately after the employee layoffs, I guarantee we would have seen data suggesting a very different culture. Instead of being caring, supportive, and people-oriented, we would have seen data and read comments suggesting POM was focused on the bottom line and didn't care about people. The reality was very different. None of the day-to-day aspects of the culture had changed. POM continued to invest heavily in programs designed to support employee well-being, engagement, and connection. In fact, they increased spending in these areas after the layoffs, recognizing the negative effect this would have on morale, productivity, and engagement. In this case, the culture remained the same, but the climate changed.

The culture survey my company offers also measures organizational climate, or people's experience of the culture. It is different in that we analyze and interpret the survey results in context to reveal insights into the company's values and belief system. This contextual analysis also allows us to identify the cultural strengths that should be protected and built upon as well as the changes leaders might want to consider to better align their culture with their strategy. By contrast, most culture surveys provide data instead of insights. It is left to human resources to analyze the data and engage leaders to decide on a course of action. This can result in the understandable mistake of failing to consider context and the relationship between a company's culture and strategy and instead focusing on the low scores or gaps identified in the survey results. While interpreting results in context can be learned with training and experience, if you are new to the field of culture, it is worthwhile to engage a culture expert to assist you the first time you work with assessment results. Better yet, seek out an expert who is willing to transfer knowledge to you and others so you are ready and able to do this yourself in the future.

CHANGING CULTURE, PART TWO: PROGRESS STALLS

When we left off in part one, Diane and Tom had developed an action plan based on the culture assessment findings. Over the months that followed, Tom and his team worked hard to improve the company's core business processes with the active involvement of frontline employees, their supervisors, and their managers. They also provided extensive training on Lean Six Sigma principles and practices. The training was mandatory for all employees and managers, including the leadership team, although the latter's training was less technical, with an emphasis on their role in leading change and building a Lean Six Sigma culture. Concurrently, Diane's HR team redesigned roles and responsibilities, updated the company's competency model with new behaviors, and made the promised changes to people processes. They also assisted Tom in implementing an exhaustive multipronged communication strategy engaging leaders to help build employee awareness of the changes and why they were needed and keep employees up-to-date on what was happening.

Fast-forward eighteen months and Tom was preparing to meet with the executive team to provide a progress report that was to include the Lean Six Sigma initiative's preliminary performance data. Diane asked me to assist by rerunning the culture assessment with the same sixty questions used previously. When Diane and I looked at the results, it was clear there had been little change, if any. The good news was that employee engagement and commitment to the company remained very strong, despite the changes employees had seen and continued to experience. However, a close look at process discipline, which was the dimension Tom was most interested in, revealed that a significant percentage of employees believed that the company's processes were more of a guideline than a rule and that it was okay to deviate from them if they felt there was a better way to do things. Furthermore, they believed that process improvement efforts were less effective than before Lean Six Sigma.

Given the work Tom and his team had done, we expected that he would be disappointed and maybe even frustrated or angry when we shared our findings with him. But in fact, he was not the least bit surprised and quickly turned the discussion to how he could use the survey results to address some problems his team had been experiencing. He went on to explain that from day one, they had met with a lot of resistance, especially within operations, which was the department most affected by the change. Initially, the resistance came from the employees who were afraid that this change would mean more layoffs and older employees losing their jobs to younger people with up-to-date skills. It took a lot of conversations over a few months for them to believe this wasn't going to happen and start contributing to the process redesign effort. However, this work was also met with resistance because the employees rebelled against the idea of standard processes. To them, this meant they would lose the flexibility and the freedom to do things the way they believed was best. Despite this, the work was eventually completed, and Tom's team, with HR's help, moved on to redefining roles and responsibilities. Once again, they encountered resistance, this time from managers who recognized they were also going to have to, in their words, "be the compliance police" and would no longer have the same freedom to use their discretion and exercise their judgment.

Training, Tom said, was also a problem. First off, the senior leadership team decided that they could only be available for one two-hour workshop instead of the two-and-a-half-day training normally provided to executives. Then, two of the executives dropped out at the last minute. They told Tom this was because of urgent business demands, although he suspected they thought the training wasn't relevant and were looking for an excuse. When he asked the COO to intervene, he was told not to force the issue, as their participation wasn't critical. This was despite Tom pointing out that the executives were expected to introduce and fully participate in the training provided to their teams. This trend to allow people to opt out of the training became a recurring problem, especially with managers and employees of the groups outside of operations. As for the leaders who had not attended the workshop, Tom almost wished they had found a reason not to attend their team's training either. Instead of being champions of the new initiative and showing their support, they asked questions that challenged why the company was spending so much money on it and raised objections, such as why their team was involved when this was obviously an operations initiative.

Frustrating as this was, the other and even more important issue Tom highlighted was the behavior of the leaders, including some executives. Beyond the problems with training, there were numerous examples of leaders undermining the efforts of the Lean Six Sigma team. The most egregious was allowing people to deviate from the Lean Six Sigma processes. This began early on in the implementation of the new processes and had increased in frequency in recent months. From what his team had been able to ascertain, the message from senior leaders to managers and employees was that the new processes were intended to reduce waste and improve efficiency. However, they still expected people to use their judgment and, if they saw a better way to do things, do it. This was in direct conflict with one of the principal tenets of Lean Six Sigma, which is to reduce process variation and, in so doing, improve quality and lower operating costs. It also conflicted with the commitment the senior leadership team had made to fully support the change effort. Early on, they had discussed the fact that Lean Six Sigma was going to be a significant change and that it was likely to be met with resistance. To be successful, senior leaders needed to make it clear through their words and actions that they fully supported Tom and his team, especially when things got tough. Yet, this was not happening.

To illustrate, Tom told me about a recent staff meeting he attended with managers from the operations team. The mid-level manager leading the meeting asked each manager to provide an update and identify any specific challenges they wanted to discuss. It quickly became apparent that the managers were unhappy with the new standardized processes and wanted the okay to go back, at least somewhat, to the way things had been done before Lean Six Sigma. When Tom interjected to suggest that employees needed more time to adjust to the new processes and there would be plenty of opportunities to improve them in the future, the managers quickly and loudly disagreed. The problem, they said, was not with the process design but the fact that they were standardized and that compliance without exception was required. They went on to say that this was not realistic, as problems occurred all the time that needed to be fixed quickly and required the knowledge gained from experience. Equipment breakdowns were one example, materials shortages another, and employee absenteeism was a third. The list went on. Furthermore, they said, while they understood the end-to-end process might improve things, they were skeptical.

By taking away the ability to make small adjustments that they knew from experience would produce a better outcome, their part of the process was not as effective as it had been.

The midlevel manager sat silently throughout the discussion. When he saw that they had reached a stalemate, he told the managers that he expected them to make sure there was a very good reason not to follow the Lean Six Sigma process; however, if this could be established, it was okay to allow some variation. With that, the meeting ended, and the managers left the room happy. As Tom approached him to question his decision, the midlevel manager raised his hand to cut him off. He told Tom that he understood his concerns; however, his team needed time to adjust and Tom must admit that the new processes were far from perfect. The next day, Tom decided to check what was happening on the shop floor. As he expected, the word had quickly gotten out, and he heard employees telling others not to worry about following the new process. Their manager had told them they could go back to the way they'd done things before.

This brings us back to the results of the culture assessment and the upcoming meeting with the leadership team to report on the progress of the Lean Six Sigma initiative. Despite the extensive communication and training managers and employees had received, they were not getting the message. If this continued, the entire initiative was at risk of failing and the company would have wasted five million dollars. The only solution, Tom believed, was for leaders, starting with executives, to enforce compliance and stop allowing exceptions. Tom realized his boss might take this as a personal criticism, given he was the head of operations; however, he didn't see another option. Working together, Tom, Diane, and I developed a strategy that we believed had a reasonable chance of success. We decided it would be better if I, a neutral outside party, presented the culture assessment results. Tom would follow with the financials and segue into a facilitated discussion of why the initiative was not achieving its targets. The hope was that by taking this approach, the COO and the rest of the leadership team would be less defensive and more open to exploring solutions.

Lesson #14—Communication and change management aren't enough.

Tom and Diane did the right things the right way using the tools available within their sphere of influence. Yet, despite this, they were unable to overcome manager and employee resistance to the change. The cultural defensive routines were too strong and widespread. The only way these could be conquered was if senior leaders were to consistently and actively show they were personally committed to the changes Tom was introducing with Lean Six Sigma. They needed to walk the talk. When senior leaders and midlevel managers chose to continue to say and do things the way they had in the past, they reinforced the status quo and undermined the Lean Six Sigma change effort. It didn't matter if they said they supported Lean Six Sigma or attended the training, managers and employees recognized the truth: their leaders did not believe in the changes the company was implementing. They only said they supported them because they knew that to do otherwise was career suicide.

We predicted this would happen. Tom and Diane recognized that the changes being introduced with Lean Six Sigma were not going to be popular with employees, especially when they followed so closely on the heels of the company's first-ever employee layoff. They knew that employees at all levels valued the flexibility and freedom they had to do things the way they felt was best. They also believed that this had contributed to the company's past success. They also knew that Lean Six Sigma was going to require compliance with defined processes and procedures, which employees were not going to like. The culture survey had also highlighted some challenges with collaboration, communication, and candor. This meant they could not assume that the dialogue needed to build understanding and commitment to the changes was going to happen organically, especially given the resistance they were seeing from senior leaders and other managers. The one piece of good news that provided some hope was the strong score on employee engagement. Employees at every level genuinely cared about the company and wanted it to succeed.

With this in mind, Diane and her HR team, in consultation with Tom, designed a comprehensive communication and change management strategy to support the implementation of Lean Six Sigma. Their approach emphasized employee engagement and the positive relationships that existed between employees and their immediate managers. By engaging employees, the hope was that they would feel their concerns and ideas had been heard and given serious consideration. At the same time, the dialogue that took place would build understanding of the reasons for the changes, and with this would come acceptance that supporting them was in the best interest of the company and employees.

They also realized that the effectiveness of their approach depended on the managers who would implement it. To this end, they provided managers with training and a comprehensive suite of communication and change management tools. It would have been hard to find a better example of communication and change management anywhere. Yet, despite their best efforts, the Lean Six Sigma initiative was in trouble, in large part due to the company's inability to overcome resistance and align its culture with its strategy. To be clear, this is a "yes and" versus an "either/or" situation. Communication and change management are essential to the success of any change effort. They are not sufficient, however, if the objective is to change a company's culture. But we'll get into that later.

Lesson #15 — Behavioral approaches are good but not enough.

When Diane told Tom that HR would support Lean Six Sigma by identifying, with his input, new expected behaviors and embedding these in their practices and processes, she advocated the behavioral approach to culture change. This is one of the most popular culture change strategies currently used by organizations. The main premise of the behavioral approach is that we can change culture by changing behavior. In other words, if everyone consistently follows core work processes instead of doing things the way they think is best, we will build a more process-oriented culture. Similarly, if people openly voice their opinions, ideas, questions, and concerns, we will build a culture that is more open and transparent.

With the behavioral approach, the first step is usually to clearly define the company's desired culture or its values. This anchors the identification of expected behaviors, which are the behaviors we will see when the company has the culture it needs to execute its strategy and achieve its goals. A competency model based on the desired culture or company values is an example of this. For example, what behaviors will we see at POM when we have built a culture that embodies process discipline and execution excellence? These behaviors are then embedded into talent acquisition, performance management, rewards and recognition, employee development, and perhaps even career advancement and succession planning practices. This effort is often accompanied by communication and education initiatives designed to fast-track adoption of the desired behaviors.

Once again, Diane did what she thought was the right and best way to achieve the culture change needed to support the transition to Lean Six Sigma. This was absolutely the right thing to do. Employees need to know what is expected of them in terms of their behavior and why this is important. This must be reinforced by HR policies, practices, and processes, as these are some of the most powerful levers available to create the conditions for successful culture change. These are all things you as an HR/OD professional can do to support and accelerate the change effort. The problem is that, on its own, this is not enough. As we saw from POM's experience, the behavioral approach did not result in the needed culture change within the time frame required to achieve the company's goals. This was because of the disconnect between the words and actions of leaders and the behaviors that HR identified and embedded in its processes. It was unsuccessful despite the changes to processes, roles, responsibilities, performance metrics, and so on. While the environmental conditions were in place to encourage and reinforce new behaviors, this was trumped by the lack of coherence between the words and actions of leaders.

Lesson #16 — Grassroots movements are also good but not enough.

Diane and Tom recognized the importance of involving employees in the change effort, especially given the level of employee engagement at POM. As a result, they made sure to intentionally build employee consultation and participation into their plans. Employees expected their managers and senior leaders to ask for their opinions and suggestions whenever a change was considered. The fact that they were not consulted on the decision to implement Lean Six Sigma was a sore point. If they were not involved in the change effort, there would have been an even greater degree of resistance than what occurred. This would have doomed Lean Six Sigma to fail regardless of any other actions taken.

I raise this issue because you may have heard that the best way to change culture is to create a grassroots movement, which is basically a high-engagement approach popular with many HR professionals and consultants. The design of grassroots culture change initiatives varies; however, they are based on the premise that organizations can accelerate culture change by deeply engaging employees early and often in the change effort. The belief is that when other employees hear their peers talking about the change and see positive things happening, they will jump on board, thereby creating a movement that leads to rapid adoption of new behaviors and ways of working. Obviously, this has merit, and if you have the resources, it is worth considering as part of your change effort.

In a typical grassroots approach, a representative group of employees works together over a period of months or longer on a culture change initiative. These employees are usually given a title such as "culture champions" or a "culture committee."

This role is usually in addition to their other responsibilities, which can be a challenge given competing work demands. In the first phase, these champions help leaders identify the culture the organization needs to achieve its goals and compare this to their experience of the current culture to identify where there are important differences. In the next phase, the culture champions build on this work to recommend actions to close the gaps. Their ideas are shared with senior leaders, who review the culture champions' recommendations and make decisions on how to move forward. This work gets further developed into a clear action plan that senior leaders sign off on and the culture champions help implement. The culture champions continue to meet throughout the implementation phase to share lessons learned and identify other changes needed.

As with the behavioral approach, a grassroots movement can help to accelerate culture change; however, on its own, it is rarely successful. In my experience, most of these efforts lose energy as other pressing demands are given higher priority. When this happens, employees get reassigned to other work and the amount of time they are allowed to engage in the initiative is severely limited. Similarly, senior leaders whose role is to steward the change process lose focus and direct their energy elsewhere.

All this is to say that engaging employees in a meaningful way is important to the success of any culture change effort. This cannot, however, replace the personal ownership and active involvement of leaders. The effort also needs to be planned and managed to optimize employee involvement, as it is rare for an organization to have enough spare resources available to dedicate employees to initiatives of this kind. In most cases, employees are asked to take on culture work in addition to their other responsibilities or, if their tasks are redistributed to colleagues, expected to handle an increased workload. This can cause resentment and is rarely sustainable for longer than a few weeks at the most. Even if the work is distributed, it is common for managers to set conditions that limit the participation of their employees, such as they are only available one half-day a month or can only attend a couple of workshops. These are only a few examples of the problems you can expect to deal with if you attempt to change culture by using a grassroots approach.

With all this in mind, let's get back to our story.

CHANGING CULTURE, PART THREE: LEADERSHIP INTERVENTION

The meeting with the leadership team went even better than planned, with the CEO voicing his concerns and emphasizing the importance of being fully committed to Lean Six Sigma. The company was investing a lot of money and depending on the resulting cost savings to achieve its financial goals and, ultimately, save jobs. If this didn't happen, deep cuts were going to be needed, which would affect everyone. The message was clear: he expected every member of the leadership team to get on board, and there were to be no exceptions.

He then admitted to making a mistake by agreeing to a two-hour training program instead of the recommended two-and-a-half-days. Obviously, this was not sufficient, and he was going to correct it, starting now. He asked Tom to work with his assistant to schedule the training and told the other executives that he expected every one of them to attend. He did not want to hear any excuses. He then told them that they were to immediately start meeting with managers and employees and let them know that they were to follow the new processes as designed as well as any other practices required as part of Lean Six Sigma. Tom and his team were to wait one week for the message to get out and then start monitoring compliance and provide him with a weekly report of their findings. He made it very clear that any executive who failed to follow his direction would be answerable to him.

A few months later, I reconnected with Tom, and he told me that things had improved. The leadership team had completed the training, and the number of deviations from processes was down significantly. He was optimistic that they had turned the corner and that people were beginning to see the value of the initiative. That said, he was concerned that the real issue behind the resistance had not been addressed. People were complying because they feared losing their jobs, not because they believed in what they were doing. This was not good for morale, and he was worried employee engagement was on the decline and POM would start to lose good people. I suggested perhaps the problem was that, though the CEO had mandated different behavior, he and the rest of the leadership team had not addressed the root cause of why people were resisting.

I reminded him this was an old company with a lot of long-tenured employees who had always had the freedom to use their discretion and judgment in doing their jobs. This had helped the company to be successful and was ingrained in the company's culture and identity. Lean Six Sigma threatened this by insisting on process compliance and doing things in a specified way. Of course they were going to resist. Employees were experiencing the loss of the freedom and flexibility they valued. Maybe with time, they would accept the new way of working, but until this happened, Tom was correct in anticipating that there would be morale problems that had the potential to negatively affect performance and productivity. It was also reasonable to expect some turnover of employees as people sought other work opportunities that could meet their needs. This is why the change management, employee engagement, and communication initiatives that Diane was leading, which he was helping to implement, were so crucial. While it was extremely difficult, if not impossible, to eliminate the risk of attrition and a decline in morale, it was important to limit the damage as much as possible and keep it to the shortest time frame.

I also reminded Tom that, though the freedom and flexibility employees so valued and craved created challenges, attempting to eliminate this would be ill-advised. Instead, I suggested he and Diane think about how this could be redirected in a positive and productive manner. I went on to explain that this freedom and flexibility made it possible to quickly resolve urgent problems, create an exceptional customer experience, identify ways to do things better, and generate new ideas, among other advantages. I told him many companies that were even more process-oriented struggle to accomplish this, with my message being that instead of trying to eliminate it, they should try to protect and leverage it. Tom and Diane's challenge was to achieve the balance between freedom and flexibility and the process orientation that was needed to execute their strategy and achieve their goals. Again, this is a matter of "yes and," not "either/or."

Lesson #17—Mandating culture change does not work, period.

This entire story has been about how Diane, the HR leader, led the culture change effort at POM. Tom was involved; however, his focus was on the process and other changes required to implement Lean Six Sigma. The other leaders were participants, completing tasks such as attending employee training and engaging in communication. In the end, the CEO intervened and used his authority to mandate change.

If you are thinking, *Okay, this is the secret to culture change*, I'm sorry, but you're wrong. Mandating culture change does not work, period. While you might see some immediate progress that leads you to believe all is well, I guarantee this is temporary. The problem with mandated change is that it doesn't address beliefs. When beliefs remain unchanged, behaviors and decisions will eventually regress to align with what people believe is best and right. In other words, they will go back to the way things were before. In some cases, mandated change can also cause passive or overt resistance and create issues with employee morale and engagement that negatively affect productivity and performance. In extreme cases, this can even result in people intentionally sabotaging the change effort.

As I stated before, the only way culture change is successful is when leaders, starting at the top, personally own and are actively involved and committed to the change. Everything else flows from there. The problem, in my experience, is that this rarely happens. Culture, for reasons stated previously, is assumed to be HR's responsibility, freeing leaders to deal with the other demands of the business. The reason the needed change to a more process-oriented culture happened at POM was that senior leaders eventually led the way by demonstrating, through their words and actions, that they believed in and supported the change. Without this, the efforts of Tom, Diane, and their teams would have yielded limited results, if any.

So, where does this leave us?

In this chapter and the previous two chapters, I have shared many of the lessons I learned over my years working with organizations to understand and change culture. Many of these lessons pointed out things that work, and others revealed things to avoid. Ultimately, however, it was only recently I had an experience that finally provided the answer to my career-long quest to understand how to achieve meaningful and sustained culture change in organizations. It is this experience that I share in the next chapter.

CHAPTER FOUR
THE MISSING PIECE

THE CHIEF HUMAN RESOURCES officer (CHRO) of a large tele-communications company once memorably told me he wished there was another word for *culture*. When I asked why, he explained that senior leaders view culture as vague, warm, and fuzzy, as an HR thing. He went on to say it was impossible to get them to see culture as a business priority requiring the same level of attention as, say, achieving financial results, improving business processes, or developing strategic plans.

My solution, at the time, was to double down on finding evidence that would convince leaders they were wrong, that culture is just as important as other business priorities, if not more so. After all, who can argue with the evidence, especially given that respected experts such as John Kotter and James Heskett were reporting a direct link between corporate culture and performance?[12]

Guess what happened? No matter how strong the evidence or how compelling my argument, I could not convince leaders to see culture as a business priority worthy of their personal time and attention. Then one day, something unexpected happened. I realized what was missing. The missing piece, the key to getting to the next level and really making a difference, came unexpectedly when I was asked to help improve the effectiveness of an executive team.

CONFLICT AT A HIGH-TECH COMPANY

The chief people officer (CPO) at an advanced video solutions company—hereafter referred to as AVSC—contacted me to do team effectiveness work with its executives. She explained that over the past year, relationships on the executive team had become increasingly tense to the point that it was dysfunctional. Meetings were unproductive, decisions weren't being made, and there was finger-pointing and blaming. The list of dysfunctional behaviors went on and on. The CEO—who we will refer to as Terry—had tried to address the situation but with no success, which is why the CPO called me.

When I asked what they had tried to address the situation, the CPO—who we will refer to as Sarah—said her HR team had provided the executives with training on how to hold difficult conversations and hired an outside mediator to help the team navigate their differences. She had personally intervened by meeting with each executive to understand their perspectives and offer advice. She had also tried to facilitate some of their meetings but quickly gave up when it became apparent they weren't open to her acting in this role. The CEO, Terry, had also met with each executive one-on-one and read them the riot act regarding their behavior and the need to put aside their differences and work together. For a short while after these meetings, things had gotten better, but it didn't last. Things were just as bad as before, if not worse. The bottom line was that nothing had worked, which is why she was speaking with me.

The Executives' Perspective of the Situation

Over the next few weeks, I interviewed the members of the executive team, with the intent to get a better understanding of the situation. As I listened, it became clear we were dealing with much more than dysfunctional team dynamics. The company was struggling to achieve its financial targets. Revenues had flatlined for three years, while operating costs had increased, and profits were down. The leaders explained this was, in part, a product of the nature of their business. The company made money by licensing its intellectual property (IP) to other companies. Most licenses were for five-year terms, and several of these were in midterm. The problem was that AVSC wasn't signing new customers. The company had historically concentrated its sales and marketing efforts on the North American market, which had reached a saturation point. To continue to grow, it had to break into new markets in Europe, the Middle East, and Africa (EMEA) as well as the Asia Pacific (APAC), where it didn't have established relationships or a strong brand identity. They then explained this was partially what was behind the dynamics among the executive team.

The executive team, especially the sales, business development, and corporate strategy leaders, were under a lot of pressure to deliver financial results. These executives, and some of their peers, believed that they needed to be much more aggressive in the way they approached the EMEA and APAC markets. This meant being willing to use pressure tactics, move fast, and take some risks when dealing with customers in these markets. The problem was that the company's general counsel (GC)—whom we will call Nicholas—did not agree, and he apparently had the CEO's support, as Terry did nothing to contradict him. Nicholas was adamant that they avoid doing anything that could potentially be a problem in future negotiations. He also strongly believed that it was in the company's best interests to stay out of the courts and avoid litigation whenever possible. The result was that the company was risk-averse, cautious, and slow, which customers were using to their advantage.

The executives went on to explain that, while they respected Nicholas, they were not enamored with the extent of legal's influence in the company. To paraphrase, one person even described Nicholas and his team as empire-building gatekeepers preventing the people who made money for the company from doing their jobs. One executive provided an example where she needed to hire a contractor to help her team handle a spike in their workload. It took a month and several iterations and revisions before she finally had a contract from legal that she could act on. In the meantime, the initiative she needed the contractor's help with was already a month behind schedule. Another executive described how he couldn't even do something minor, such as rent a meeting room at a hotel, without legal's approval, which often took weeks. Another talked about how he tried to speed things up by using a contract legal had prepared in the past but even this went through several revisions and took a long time to finalize. There was example after example.

The solution, most of the executives suggested, was to reduce Nicholas's authority and allow them to make decisions and do their jobs with significantly less legal oversight. After all, they were executives and hoped that Terry and the board of directors (BOD) trusted that they knew what they were doing and would act in the company's best interests. If not, as one person suggested, they should all be fired, and the BOD should find a new team to replace them. To them, the fact that they couldn't do anything involving a customer or a contract without legal's involvement bordered on the absurd. They went on to explain that if Nicholas and his team had less power, it would free the company to be more aggressive in the pursuit of new business.

They would be able to move faster and take some risks, resulting in more sales and increased revenues. While they recognized this could lead to an increase in customer litigation, they believed that this was acceptable given the financial pressure the company was under. Their frustration was palpable.

Legal's Perspective of the Situation

When I met Nicholas, he had been with the company for about fifteen years and had worked his way up the corporate ladder from an assistant attorney to his current executive position as AVSC's general counsel. Despite their frustration with his policies, everyone I spoke with indicated how much they liked and respected Nicholas as a person and a leader. They described him as incredibly smart and accomplished, yet he was humble, hardworking, and unquestionably had the company's best interests at heart. However, the latter also translated into strong views as to what he felt was best and right for the company.

As Nicholas explained, when he was promoted to his role as GC, the BOD made it clear that his mandate was to protect the company from harm. This meant keeping it out of the courts and out of trouble with government regulators. They also told him to be vigilant and keep an eye on the sales team. He explained that this wasn't a criticism of the sales team so much as the BOD recognizing how difficult it was to close deals. Their customers either didn't want to pay for the license to use AVSC's IP or, if they were forced to do so, tried to pay as little as possible. To achieve their ends, customers used every means at their disposal to negotiate an advantageous contract and were willing, if necessary, to litigate their case in the courts. The BOD knew this, which led them to believe that sales, whose compensation was largely incentive-based and tied to revenue generation, might decide to do something to get a deal done that would come back to haunt the company in future negotiations and litigation.

Nicholas took the BOD's mandate seriously. He believed that the best way to execute this was to manage the small things so the big things looked after themselves. He explained that while it might seem excessive to require that a lawyer review a contract to rent a meeting room, doing so made sure that legal was involved in other more important things. In his experience, people looked for any excuse to bypass legal, and this was the best way to prevent that from happening. Nicholas emphasized his point by quoting multiple instances where, without legal's scrutiny, the sales team would have done something that would have caused a problem for the company. This is why he insisted that a lawyer be involved in every customer interaction and review and approve every document sent by sales to third parties. By doing so, the lawyers acquired first-hand information they used to advise sales during contract negotiations and ensure written documents were accurate and complete. This also allowed the lawyers to check that sales was not saying or doing something that could undermine the company's position in future negotiations and court cases.

When I asked Nicholas what he had to say with regard to the accusations that legal was impeding growth with its policy of zero risk tolerance, he became defensive. He was adamant that the policies he had put in place were in the company's best interests. He reiterated that this was his primary responsibility as GC. He pointed out that his team helped, not hindered, sales' ability to get deals signed that were in the company's favor, referencing the counsel they provided during negotiations and the quality of the contracts they prepared, among other things.

Furthermore, he said that sales was trying to put the blame on legal for their own incompetence and inability to deliver the results the company needed.

The CEO's Perspective of the Situation

Now, you might be wondering why Terry didn't simply tell Nicholas and the legal department they needed to do things differently, which is what the other executives inferred was required. The answer was that, first of all, Terry respected Nicholas and valued his counsel. Second, the BOD had repeatedly emphasized that they expected Terry and Nicholas to protect the company's best interests, which included keeping it out of the courts and preventing sales from doing something that could damage its future negotiating position. Terry was reluctant to do or say anything that conflicted with this mandate.

While he agreed with the other executives to an extent, Terry felt that the executive team needed to find a way to do both—aggressively pursue new business and protect the company's best interests. He believed that the only way this was going to happen was for everyone on the executive team to reconcile their differences and work together to arrive at a mutually agreeable solution. He recognized that this wasn't going to be easy. However, he also believed that there was no way they were going to make any progress unless this was addressed, which is why he asked Sarah to find someone to help. That person was me, and he sincerely hoped I was up to the task.

My response was to say that while I believed I could help, I wanted the chance to observe the executive team in action and see the dynamics for myself before I agreed to anything. Terry agreed and suggested I attend an upcoming strategy meeting. He selected this meeting because the team would be discussing the challenges the company was experiencing in closing deals in EMEA and APAC. This would be the fifth or sixth meeting to discuss the topic, and he expected things to get heated. He guaranteed I would see exactly what he and Sarah were talking about.

My Observation of the Executive Team

A week later, I found myself at the back of the room, observing the executives go at it. As expected, there was a lot of finger-pointing and blaming, most of it directed at Nicholas and his legal team, whose actions, it was suggested, played into the delay tactics being used by EMEA and APAC customers and their lawyers. Nicholas was, understandably, defensive and reminded the other executives that his team's job was to keep the company out of harm's way, which included staying out of the courts. Basically, the entire two hours were spent with each side advocating their position using increasingly heated language until the chief strategy officer (CSO) decided he had heard enough and left the room. Meeting over.

Throughout the entire meeting, I watched Terry, who said very little until the end, when, after the CSO left, one of the executives turned to him and asked what he was going to do to resolve the situation. The executive, who was obviously very frustrated and agitated, stated, and I paraphrase, that continuing the discussion was a waste of time and would get them nowhere. They were at an impasse, and Terry needed to do something about it. Terry's response was that this wasn't going to happen. They were going to continue to meet until they came up with a solution that everyone in the room could agree to. He then told them that the discussion would continue tomorrow and the day after that and the day after that until an agreement was made. With that, he left the room.

Finding a Path Forward

I met with Terry and Sarah after the meeting to share my observations and discuss next steps. I began by explaining that I understood why he and Sarah believed that the team was dysfunctional and that they needed to invest in team effectiveness work. I agreed that there was merit to this, as the behaviors I observed and the frustration and resentment that was behind them meant the executives were not having the quality discussion and debate required to move forward. They were stuck, and from what I had seen, this was likely spilling over into other topics and affecting their teams. Sarah confirmed this, noting that several employees had come to HR complaining about the toxic behavior of some of the executives. Her team had also recently shared that they were increasingly hearing about problems among different teams, many of them involving legal.

It was at this point that I suggested that handling this situation the same as most team effectiveness initiatives was unlikely to get at the root cause of the problem and lead to sustainable change. Certainly, I could introduce practices to encourage respectful dialogue and address the dysfunctional behavior. I could help the executives understand one another's styles and learn how to communicate better. Using the principles of polarity management, I could also help them better understand and appreciate the merits of others' perspectives and possibly find common ground. I could even provide coaching and mediate conflicts between the leaders and their teams. The problem was that all these things, while helpful, would only provide temporary relief. The pressure from the BOD and the market was not going away anytime soon and, I suspected, was likely to increase until the problem the company faced was resolved.

As a result, the executives would be even more stressed and revert, sooner rather than later, to their old behavior.

The challenge was that every executive was acting with the best of intentions. While their behavior might be suspect, the positions they advocated were grounded in the genuine belief that they were doing what was best and right for the company. The sales team believed that to close deals in EMEA and APAC, the company needed to move faster, be more aggressive, and take risks. Nicholas did not support the sales team's solution because he believed it could harm the company, which was in direct conflict with the mandate given to him by the BOD. The rest of the executives supported the sales solution because they believed that the company could not succeed by continuing to do things the way it had in the past. While Terry's frustration with the team's inability to find a path forward was understandable, expecting them to abandon or change their deeply held beliefs—which, again, were motivated by their commitment to do what was in the best interests of the company—was unfair and unrealistic. Of course, he could always decide to tell Nicholas to support the majority's decision; however, doing so came with the very real risk that Nicholas would decide to quit, which would create other problems.

Instead, I suggested that Terry meet with Nicholas and have a frank conversation about his expectations of him as a member of the executive team, not just the company's GC. I went on to explain that, from what I had heard and observed, Nicholas viewed his role as being limited to legal. He did not understand that as a member of the company's executive team, he had to wear two hats. One was that of a functional leader, which he wore very well, and the other was that of an enterprise business leader, which was where improvement was needed.

Nicholas, as well as every other member of the executive team, was accountable for achieving AVSC's goals and financial targets. This meant that he needed to engage fully, not just as the company's GC, in finding a solution to the company's current financial problems. It wasn't enough for him to simply veto others' ideas, even when he had reason to do so. He needed to offer suggestions, ask questions, and work with the other members of the team to find a solution. If this meant that legal needed to change some of its policies, then it was important that Nicholas knew he would have Terry's full support to do so, especially in managing any objections raised by the BOD. Using this approach, Terry could respect and acknowledge the efficacy of Nicholas's beliefs while at the same time helping him understand that the situation had changed, and as a result, he may need to consider the possibility that his beliefs regarding what was best for the company may also need to change.

When I checked back with Sarah the following week, she told me that Terry had met with Nicholas—a surprise to her, because Terry avoided conflict and tough conversations. From what she could tell, it went well, and it appeared that Nicholas listened. At the next strategy meeting, the executives, with Nicholas's input, made a breakthrough, agreeing to a significant change to the company's strategy. There was considerable debate and some dissent, but ultimately, a decision was made that all executives supported. As a team, they agreed to move forward with a new strategy that involved initiating litigation to apply pressure on EMEA and APAC customers to sign deals. They also agreed that instead of avoiding government regulators, they would aggressively lobby for policy changes.

All the executives recognized that the success of the new strategy depended on Nicholas and his legal team, as they were responsible for both litigation and regulatory affairs. Nicholas rightfully interpreted this as a vote of confidence. It helped that the CEO and his peers acknowledged that the way legal had operated was a big part of the company's past success. They were doing the right thing by protecting the company's interests; however, things had changed, and the company's survival required that they do things differently. Nicholas and his legal team could hold their heads high.

Nicholas's endorsement of the new strategy was a giant step forward, as it meant he supported taking risks, being aggressive, and acting quickly. This led him to initiate several changes that affected the way the legal team operated. While his belief in his mandate to protect AVSC from harm had not changed fundamentally, he made an important shift. He recognized that legal needed to balance protecting the interests of the company with implementing policies that allowed it to take some risks in the pursuit of new business. In effect, Nicholas and the other executives agreed the culture that had served the company so well in the past had become a problem and needed to change.

Lesson #18—We need to ask the right questions.

Prior to my interactions with Nicholas, I had assumed leaders like him must not be aware of their beliefs and how these influence their behavior, decisions, and the people around them. After all, what leader would knowingly act in a way that would cause a problem for the business? If they were aware, wouldn't they have made the changes that were needed?

I was wrong.

Nicholas was fully aware of his beliefs and how these influenced his behavior, policy decisions, and other actions. He knew exactly what he was doing and why he was doing it. Even with the rest of the executive team telling him that his policies were causing problems for the company, he refused to change. He genuinely believed that what he was doing was right—he was protecting the company's interests and, in doing so, fulfilling the mandate given to him by the BOD.

Upon reflection, I realized that when leaders behave in a certain way, even if others see this as a problem, there is almost always a good reason. They are doing what they believe is best and right for the organization. Hence, it is important to assume positive motives and intentions, except on the rare occasion when a leader behaves unethically, abuses the power of their position, or causes harm. In these situations, it is important to act swiftly and decisively, which, in many cases, means terminating the leader or putting them on notice at the very least. If this doesn't happen, we send the message that toxic behavior is condoned by the company, which has negative consequences for the culture and the company. Fortunately, in my experience, these cases are the rare exception, and the vast majority of leaders and employees have the company's best interests at heart.

That is to say, no wonder we have been stymied in our efforts to convince leaders to personally own and be actively involved in culture change. When we talk to them about being positive role models; changing their behavior; or needing to make changes to policies, practices, or programs, we've missed the mark. All we've done is demonstrate to the leader that we don't understand their situation or respect their perspective, motives, and capabilities. If the leader believes what they are doing is the right thing for the organization, and their behavior and actions are based on this, we are not going to convince them to change simply by telling them to do so.

So, what is the answer?

I went back and reviewed my notes from my interviews with the executives. The company had a major business problem that was caused in large part by its risk-averse culture. The leaders pointed to Nicholas and his legal team as the reason for the culture and the cause of the problem, expecting that Terry would force the changes they believed were needed. This was not going to happen. They were stuck. That was when I realized what I had missed. I was asking the wrong questions. The question wasn't "Why is Nicholas holding onto beliefs and behaviors that are causing a problem for the company?" Nor was it "How do we convince Nicholas to change?" The question that needed to be asked, before anything else, was "Why is the change needed?" What is the compelling reason to change the way the company has been doing things for years and which has contributed to its success?

It isn't about who needs to change; it's about why and what culture change is needed. When we focus on the why, we aren't talking about beliefs, values, or behaviors. Instead, we are talking about the business and how the culture supports or interferes with the company's ability to execute its strategy and achieve its goals. For example, Nicholas's company had, for years, concentrated its sales and marketing efforts on the North American market, where customers preferred to avoid litigation. Under these circumstances, AVSC's risk-averse culture, exemplified by legal's power and influence over negotiations, supported this strategy. However, the EMEA and APAC markets were completely different animals. Customers in these markets used delay tactics, including leveraging government regulators and the courts, to maneuver into an advantageous negotiating position. AVSC's desire to avoid litigation and not deal with regulators only fed into their plans. As a result, it took years to close deals that had taken months to reach a satisfactory conclusion in North America. A change was needed, not just to strategy but also to the company's risk-averse culture.

This is the type of culture (and business) problem that every senior leader is motivated to solve. It is important and compelling. The culture problem is serious enough to cause significant pain, which creates a shared sense of urgency. This is what makes changing the culture a priority for leaders on par with other demands for their time and attention. It should also be crystal clear that the only way the culture and business problem is going to be solved is by leaders getting personally involved. This starts with alignment.

Lesson #19 — Alignment is critical.

Leaders must be aligned in believing the company has a serious business problem that is caused by the current culture. They must also believe they share the accountability to solve it. If this is missing, we see situations like Nicholas's, where a leader with the best of intentions unknowingly contributes through his words and actions to the very problem the company needs to solve. In Nicholas's case, he viewed AVSC's strategy and financial problems as the responsibility of other executives. This was not his mandate nor his problem. While he participated in strategy meetings, he limited his involvement to making sure the other executives were aware of the legal and regulatory risks of proposed strategies. He would not, could not, and did not support strategies that threatened the BOD's mandate to protect the company from harm. Given the important role legal played in the company and the high regard in which he was held by Terry and the BOD, Nicholas basically had the power to veto any decision. This led to significant frustration within the executive team.

Until Nicholas accepted he had a responsibility, along with the other members of the executive team, to solve the business and culture problems negatively affecting AVSC's performance, nothing was going to change. This alignment creates common ground and focuses attention on what, not who, needs to change. This helps to discourage individuals from interpreting the need for change as a personal criticism, which can lead to resentment and defensiveness.

This concludes part one. In part two, we continue with AVSC's story, where we dive deeper into the culture-strategy dynamic and explore what happens when these are no longer aligned. Of course, this raises the question of what to do when this happens. The answer is that we use the CASPE culture change process. Read on to learn more.

PART TWO

CULTURE-STRATEGY ALIGNMENT AND THE CASPE APPROACH TO CULTURE CHANGE

CHAPTER FIVE

WHEN CULTURE EATS STRATEGY

IN CHAPTER ONE, I stated that organizational cultures aren't good or bad, instead, they exist for a reason. The problem is that sometimes things change and the culture that served the company so well in the past starts interfering with its ability to achieve its goals. The story of AVSC and how its risk-averse culture impeded revenue growth is just one of the many examples I've encountered over the years. When this happens, the company's culture is no longer an asset; it is a problem that needs to be solved.

A DISCONNECT BETWEEN STRATEGY AND CULTURE

The situation AVSC faced was not unusual. Companies, regardless of their industry, location, or size, must adapt their strategies to remain competitive and achieve their goals. The challenge is that no matter how great your company's strategy is, it will fail unless the culture supports it. If this alignment of culture and strategy is weak or missing, the culture becomes an anchor weighing down the company's efforts to execute its strategy, creating *culture drag*.

Diagram 5 illustrates the effect of culture drag on strategy execution. When culture and strategy are aligned, all aspects of the organization work together to support strategy execution. Assuming the strategy is the correct one and is well

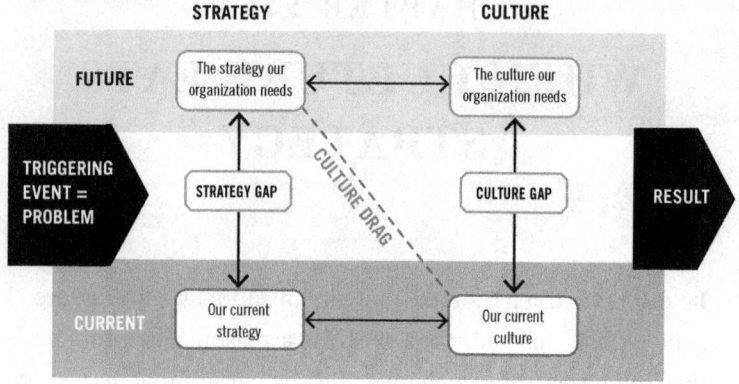

Diagram 5: Culture-strategy alignment and the effect of culture drag on strategy execution

executed, this alignment of culture and strategy helps the company achieve the outcomes it needs. When this happens, shareholders are happy, the BOD is happy, market analysts are happy, customers and suppliers are happy, and leaders and employees are happy.

Then something significant happens, *a triggering event*, and we have a problem: the company's strategy is no longer achieving its financial targets and goals. Performance declines, creating pressure to do something different. When this happens, the company experiences a *strategy gap*, which is the difference between the current strategy and the strategy the company needs to achieve its goals. If the company does nothing, the strategy gap will continue to erode performance and may eventually threaten the company's very existence. But let's say that leaders recognize the threat or opportunity the triggering event presents and initiate a change in strategy that, if executed well, will allow the company to thrive. In so doing, the strategy gap is closed, and all should be well with the world. But hold on, the culture that enabled the old strategy to be successfully executed hasn't changed; there is a *culture gap*. The company's culture has become a barrier the new strategy can't overcome, resulting in culture drag.

Until the culture changes and is aligned with the new strategy, we have a problem. The existing culture continues to eat the new strategy for breakfast, lunch, and dinner.[13]

CULTURE DRAG AT A HIGH-TECH COMPANY

To explain the dynamics of culture drag, it can be helpful to use an example, and AVSC provides an excellent one. As you may recall, for several years, AVSC had successfully executed a go-to-market strategy that was effective because it was aligned with its cautious, risk-averse culture. The company focused its efforts on building its credibility as an innovator, providing leading-edge products to other technology companies. Among other things, it sponsored and hosted highly respected and well-attended think tanks and conferences, its researchers and engineers published countless peer-reviewed articles, and it rapidly grew its catalog of patents. Protecting the value of its intellectual property was of paramount importance, resulting in an extensive volume of legal policies, procedures, and processes. While the company had initiated litigation when necessary, it preferred to avoid the costs and risks this incurred.

But then something happened . . . a triggering event.

The Triggering Event

AVSC had missed its financial targets for three straight years. What happened? Their primary market, North American technology companies, was saturated, and they were struggling to find new customers. This was the triggering event. AVSC was forced to shift its focus to the EMEA and APAC markets. While the sales team had been trying to gain traction in these markets, they had yet to sign deals of any significance. Unless the company quickly remediated the situation, there was a very real risk that external market analysts would switch AVSC from a hold to sell rating. If this happened, investors would likely pull their money out of the company, which would be devastating.

The Strategy Gap

AVSC's strategy, which had been successful in the North American market, was not working in EMEA or APAC. Specifically, while North American customers preferred to avoid litigation, their counterparts in EMEA and APAC had no such reluctance. In fact, they used litigation and, in some cases, the active involvement of government policymakers as an integral part of their negotiating strategy. This created a strategy gap, which essentially means the current strategy is not yielding the results required to achieve the organization's goals.

The New (Future) Strategy

To close the strategy gap, AVSC's executives decided to use litigation when necessary to increase the pressure on potential customers who engaged in patent infringement. In addition, they decided to actively engage external lobbyists to persuade US officials to intervene on the company's behalf in EMEA and APAC and advocate for trade policies that would put AVSC in a stronger position in these regions. The executives recognized that the work of the lobbyists was going to take time to yield results and concentrated their energy on litigation.

While there were several customer negotiations in progress, the executives agreed that it was prudent to test the new strategy before implementing it more widely. With this in mind, they selected a high-profile target in South Korea as their test case. The negotiations with this customer had been underway for over two years, in large part due to the customer's delay tactics and AVSC's desire to stay out of the courts. In addition to the obvious benefits of closing the deal and increasing revenue, the executives believed that testing the new strategy with this customer would provide insights that could be useful for future and current negotiations in the region. It would also send a message to other customers that negotiations were going to be different. AVSC was not only willing to litigate but would be aggressive in taking patent infringement cases to the courts. Importantly, it would provide evidence as to whether the new strategy worked. This proof of concept was critical, as the executives felt the need to demonstrate to the financial market and the BOD that they were in control of the situation and AVSC was back on the road to revenue growth and profitability. Confident they had landed on the right strategy, the executives quickly moved into action. Unfortunately, they didn't consider the effect the company's culture would have on strategy execution.

The Current Culture

To recap, AVSC's culture was described by most executives and employees as risk-averse, cautious, and slow-moving. This was attributed in large part to its legal policies; however, the reality was that it went much deeper. For example, every decision of even moderate consequence required extensive data gathering and analysis. As a result, it was common for decisions to take months and require countless meetings, as well as massive amounts of investigation to answer questions and test every possible scenario. This also bred a fear of getting something wrong or making a mistake, which was evident in the behavior of people at every level. Instead of using their judgment and discretion, employees deferred to their manager, effectively shifting accountability off themselves. Financial delegation of authority was also set at unusually low levels, which meant that spending decisions involving even moderate amounts of money, such as the purchase of a laptop computer for a new employee, required executive approval. Another example was the inordinate amount of effort and time spent in preparing presentations. Heaven forbid someone put a semicolon where it shouldn't be or used differently sized fonts in the titles. These are just a few examples. There were many, many more.

Boom—Culture Drag!

Despite the importance and urgency of the situation and the commitment the executive team made to aggressively pursue new business, the new strategy stalled. It couldn't break through the barriers created by the company's risk-averse culture. The culture gap was too big. In a nutshell, although legal supported the litigation strategy, they were not on board with reducing legal oversight. In fact, they doubled down on their current way of doing things, which included scrutinizing every document sent to a customer and actively participating in all customer meetings. Similarly, the executive team itself demanded an exhaustive amount of information regarding the litigation strategy and approach to negotiations, which led to weeks and months of churn. Instead of intentionally making the required changes to the culture to find an effective balance of risk and speed, behaviors didn't change, and work continued to be done the way it had in the past. This effectively put the kibosh on efforts to implement the new strategy. This is an important lesson! By not making the changes to behaviors, practices, and the organization system that were required to execute the new strategy, they doomed it to failure.

The New (Future) Culture

For AVSC's new strategy to succeed, the company needed to be more collaborative, responsive, adaptable, flexible, agile, and risk-tolerant. At the same time, the nature of AVSC's business meant that it was important to continue to protect the company from harm. This was not an "either/or" situation but rather one of "yes and." In fact, there were many other aspects of its culture that served the company well and needed to be protected and even leveraged for the company to thrive.

This included the value the company placed on people, which was evident in formal and informal aspects of organizational life. For example, employees had access to best-in-class wellness, flexible work hours, and continuing education programs. AVSC invested heavily in diversity, equity, and inclusion initiatives, which was evident in the demographic makeup of its employees, starting at the executive level. On an informal level, executives made a point of getting to know people personally, embraced an open-door policy, and did a lot of little things like sending handwritten notes to employees on birthdays or when someone did something out of the ordinary. The list went on and on. In return, AVSC's scores on its annual employee engagement survey were a benchmark for other companies in its industry. Despite the frustrations with slow decision-making and risk avoidance, employees were proud to be members of the company and wanted the opportunity to help it succeed.

Closing the Culture Gap

In an ideal world, every aspect of the way things get done in an organization—its culture—clearly supports the company's strategy. Of course, changing every facet is hardly realistic. While a broad culture change strategy is needed, tackling everything at once would take a massive investment of resources and years. This was not an option at AVSC, nor is it possible in most organizations. AVSC needed to see immediate results in the EMEA and APAC markets. This was the compelling reason for change. Addressing other manifestations of its slow, risk-averse culture, such as the waste of resources spent preparing PowerPoint presentations and the bottlenecks caused by a lack of financial delegation of authority, was not going to solve the problem. Yes, these issues would need to be addressed if they would help build the momentum needed to change the culture, but this could wait. The priority was to close the culture gap, specifically as it was manifesting in customer negotiations, and get deals signed.

AVSC opted to use an approach I developed called the CASPE culture change process (CASPE or CASPE process), which is described in detail in the following chapters. In summary, I facilitated three workshops with the executive team over a two-week period that resulted in the identification of a new customer test case and, importantly, clearly identified the changes to behaviors and practices required to drive speed and agility while at the same time minimizing the risks to the company. This was followed by joint meetings with the sales, business development, and legal teams involved in the test case negotiation, during which they refined the approach and identified obstacles that the executives agreed to address. During these meetings, the joint team, including the executives, agreed to changes to roles and responsibilities, decision-making authorities, communication practices, processes, policies, and procedures. They also discussed and agreed on the behaviors they would do their best to emulate going forward, which included how they would handle conflicts, blaming, and other behaviors that had been evident in the past. Fast-forward six months and AVSC had its first signed deal in EMEA and APAC.

Of course, this is only the first step toward culture change. Over the next three years, AVSC systematically applied the CASPE process in other parts of the business, augmenting this with a broader employee engagement strategy that capitalized on the strengths of its current culture (see chapter twelve).

Lesson #20—Culture change is about finding the right balance.

One of the challenges I observed at AVSC was the tendency of people at all levels, including the executives, to view culture as "either/or." Either the company could minimize risks or it could be decisive and agile. The reality was that, as the CEO suggested, AVSC needed balance to be successful. It needed to be aggressive while at the same time making smart decisions that would position the company well in future negotiations and litigation. This happens often in most organizations. An entrepreneurial company, like POM, that invests in Lean Six Sigma or implements a new enterprise resource planning system like SAP is faced with the challenge of maintaining the existing strengths of its culture while making changes most employees perceive as threatening to it. The result is resistance, as people default to an "either/or" mindset.

When approaching culture change, it is important people understand that you want to protect your existing strengths while at the same time finding a better balance in areas required to support strategy execution. Approaching conversations about the culture and need for change in this way can help to overcome the organization's cultural defensive routines.

Lesson #21—Triggering events are a catalyst for change.

Broadly speaking, a triggering event refers to something that has happened or is happening that forces a reaction. These can be externally initiated, as with what happened at AVSC, but they can also be internally initiated. Mergers and acquisitions, changes in senior leaders, and the implementation of new enterprise-level technology or core business processes are just a few examples of internal triggering events. A merger or acquisition fits this definition because these are directly tied to a company's growth strategy versus a direct response to something that has happened in the external environment.

External triggering events refer to things that have happened or are happening that affect the company and are outside the company's control. These types of events are happening more and more frequently as companies struggle to meet the challenges of our increasingly volatile, unpredictable, complex, and ambiguous (VUCA) world. Consider for a moment the massive external changes that have happened in recent years and continue to happen. Technological advancements are occurring at an increasing rate. Innovation in fields such as cloud computing, nanotechnology, artificial intelligence, and virtualization are putting pressure on companies to keep pace or risk losing ground to more adventurous competitors. Technological change is also affecting customers' buying patterns and preferences, as evident from the increase in consumer online purchases at the expense of brick-and-mortar sales. This has also played a major role in the rise of niche companies that use technology to provide a product or service better and faster than their less focused and bigger competitors. Geopolitical conflicts such as the US–China embargo and Russia's invasion of Ukraine have changed the parameters for doing business in these countries and others. Access to goods and materials, as well as customers, has been blocked or severely impeded, which has had a major negative impact on a significant number of companies.

Another example is the global COVID-19 pandemic that created massive disruption to the global supply chain, driving costs higher across a wide range of industries. Companies in several industries were forced to pivot or reinvent themselves or die. Take, for example, restaurants that, facing closure, changed their business model to offer takeout, home delivery, and even meal preparation packages to consumers. While this change may not last, other companies such as Spotify and Unilever made strategic changes that continue to yield results. As reported by Mauro Guillén in a 2020 *Harvard Business Review* article, Spotify offered "original content, in the form of podcasts. The platform saw artists and users upload more than 150,000 podcasts in just one month, and it has signed exclusive podcast deals with celebrities and started to curate playlists. The shift in strategy means that Spotify could become more of a tastemaker. At long last, the company is doubling down on Netflix's not-so-secret recipe for success in a business in which copyright owners enjoy healthy margins while pure-play streamers struggle to become profitable."[14]

These are just a few examples of the challenges, and occasional opportunities, created by changes in the external environment. Every company, regardless of industry or location, is affected to some extent by one or more of these events and others. It is the ability to recognize or, better yet, anticipate when this is happening and take appropriate action that determines if the organization survives or dies. Fortunately, there are companies that have not only been successful at pivoting and reinventing themselves but taken this to the next level, including Amazon, American Express, Corning, IBM, and Netflix. These companies have made reinvention a part of their culture and, in doing so, have developed a unique capability that gives them an advantage over their competitors.

Unfortunately, there are also lots of well-known stories of companies that failed to do this and are no longer in business, or if they are, they are a faint shadow of their former selves.[15] Blockbuster is a case in point. Multiple articles and case studies have been written over the years citing the company's demise as the result of its inability to adapt its business model to the threat created by Netflix and on-demand streaming services. "At its peak in 2004, Blockbuster consisted of 9,094 stores and employed approximately 84,300 people."[16] As of 2023, it operates one store in Bend, Oregon, which is more of a curiosity and tourist destination than a retail operation. Kodak, which continued to bet on its successful photographic film products despite the emergence of digital technology, is another example. BlackBerry, which at one point had eighty-five million users, reportedly failed to innovate and rapidly lost ground to Apple, Samsung, and others.[17] The list is long. In most cases, leaders underestimated or discounted the changes that were happening. The result was a strategy gap that became so great that it was insurmountable.

Now, you may be thinking, *Of course they failed. They didn't understand the changes happening in the marketplace and*

external environment and adjust their strategy accordingly.
What does it have to do with culture? This is a fair question,
but as I will explain shortly, a company's approach to strategic
planning and its choice of strategy has a lot to do with culture,
if not everything to do with it. That said, while it is rare to find
a report about a company's demise or a significant failure that
references culture as a causative factor, there are a few exceptions. The most common occurs in reference to failed mergers and acquisitions such as AT&T's 2016 acquisition of Time
Warner.[18] In this case, the differences in the cultures of the two
companies resulted in a clash that contributed to a significant
decline in AT&T's financial performance. This was despite
what appeared to be an ideal marriage of two companies with
complementary businesses: Time Warner as a content devel-
oper with a valuable inventory of related assets and AT&T as a
content distributor with a massive, established customer base.
The other exception can be found in reports of companies that
have been involved in scandals or engaged in unethical actions
that are usually attributed to the actions of senior leaders. The
Challenger space shuttle and Deepwater Horizon disasters are
two of the most famous, but there are many others, including
Enron, Barclays, Nortel, and Wells Fargo, the latter of which
was described earlier in this book.

Lesson #22—Strategy gaps are linked to culture.

In chapter one, I made the point that culture is systemic in that
it is embedded in and affects every aspect of an organization.
This includes strategy. The beliefs and values of leaders influence how the company approaches strategic planning as well as
its choice of strategy. For example, AVSC's original strategy was
a product of a formal, three-year planning process. This was a

comprehensive and rigorous effort that culminated in a three-day off-site meeting of the executive team. The objective of the meeting was to recalibrate the company's long-term goals and strategy and identify its priorities for the coming year. The meeting was jam-packed and fast-paced, taxing the energy of even the most well-rested executive. The process leading up to the meetings was also rigorous and exhaustive and involved extensive research and preparation completed by the company's five-member corporate strategy office. The CSO summarized their findings in briefing documents that were sent to the executives well in advance of the meeting. These documents included information on market dynamics, external trends, and other developments that could be a threat or potential growth opportunity for the company. The executives were expected to read the briefings carefully and use them to advance their thinking so they could make a meaningful contribution to discussions and decision-making. It was an unspoken rule that to arrive at the meeting without being fully prepared would incur the wrath of the executive vice president (EVP) of corporate strategy, and the CEO. This was something everyone wanted to avoid. After the meeting, the CSO documented the decisions that had been made in the company's formal strategic plan. When finalized, the strategic plan provided the focus for several of the company's core business processes, including goal setting, performance measurement, resource allocation and management, and compensation.

In the years between strategic planning meetings, the executives reviewed the plan on an annual basis. The principal objectives of the annual meeting were to assess the progress made toward the company's long-term goals and identify the priorities for the coming year. This also provided the opportunity to discuss emerging trends and developments in the external environment and adjust the long-term goals and strategic plan if needed. The latter only happened on very rare occasions, as any changes had to be approved by the company's BOD. The BOD had made it clear they would only agree to a change to the company's goals under exceptional circumstances. In addition to concerns about a potential negative reaction by the financial market, they believed it was important to hold the executive team accountable, which meant not moving the goalposts.

An unintended consequence of the BOD's position was that the executives were reluctant to make decisions that deviated from the plan. If a new opportunity was identified, it would get tabled until the next annual strategy meeting. This meant the company failed to act on promising new opportunities, especially ones that required a quick response. For example, the CSO once identified an opportunity to acquire a niche competitor. The team was very excited, as they had been monitoring the company for a few years in the hope that they could make a play to buy it. However, when they brought it to the executive team, they were told that a decision would have to wait until the next annual meeting. By the time this took place, the niche competitor was in the closing stages of an agreement with a competitor and the opportunity was lost.

Leaders who support this type of structured, planful approach to strategic planning typically believe it provides the focus, alignment, and accountability required to succeed. To quote Ted Jackson of ClearPoint Strategy, "It's a beautiful thing when an organization has hundreds, thousands, or even tens of thousands of employees all pulling in the same direction to achieve shared goals. When that happens, there's virtually no limit to what the business can accomplish."[19] Leaders who favor this approach believe the extensive research and analysis that accompanies the planning process is essential, as it allows for better decisions and, importantly, mitigates risk. Furthermore, they tend to view the organization as an entity with finite resources. It is incumbent on them, as leaders, to utilize these valuable and scarce resources efficiently and effectively. While there may be occasions when this means making tough choices to not invest in an exciting idea or new opportunity, it is better to focus on a few priorities and successfully complete them than to take on too much and fail to execute. This same thought process applies to opportunities that arise during the year. Allocating resources to a new opportunity requires that people, money, and other scarce resources be taken away from existing priorities. This creates the risk that one or both initiatives will not be completed or, if they are, not to the standard that is needed.

Contrast this with the strategic planning approach used by the leaders of another high-tech company that I worked with. In this company, a small team led by the EVP of corporate development (CD) constantly monitored the external environment to identify potential threats and opportunities. If something caught a team member's attention, it was researched and, if it had merit, discussed with the rest of the team. The CD team would decide if the situation or idea should be shelved, monitored, or brought forward for discussion at the executive team's monthly strategy meetings. These were carefully documented in the belief that even items that didn't have merit at the time could be potential opportunities in the future. Items to be presented to the executive team were recorded in a "strategy roster" and briefing notes were prepared. The strategy roster was a dynamic, living document the CD team updated on a continual basis.

The CD team felt this was a more effective approach than a formal, multiyear planning process given the speed and extent of change that was happening in the industry. They believed that by the time a three-year plan was developed and executed, the world would have changed, and competitors would have left the company in their dust. The company's leaders bought into the approach, sharing the belief that it would allow them to take preemptive action to address threats and take advantage of opportunities before their competitors. They also shared the belief that it was better to do something and fail than do nothing at all. They believed failures lead to better ideas and all it takes is one great idea for the company to achieve a big win. As a result, they frequently approved strategic initiatives that had a slim chance of success. In fact, one of my favorite stories was told by a software engineer at the company—whom we will refer to as Samir.

Samir had been given the go-ahead to experiment with the use of artificial intelligence (AI) in product development. He was given a small budget with the only ask being that he provide progress updates including demos to the engineering team at their regular Friday meetings. The team would evaluate his progress and decide whether there was merit in continuing his work. If the team decided to stop further work, he was expected to comply and share what he learned with other engineers to see if it would help spark an even better idea. He agreed. Everything was going smoothly until one Friday afternoon when the engineering team decided it didn't make sense to continue with his project. While he was disappointed, he understood and accepted the decision.

A month later, Samir was invited to participate in one of the company's quarterly innovation labs. The innovation labs were a big deal, as they provided an opportunity for the brightest minds in the company to get together with external thought leaders and talk about the future, share ideas, and experiment. One of the areas discussed was the future of AI and the opportunities it could create for the company. To say he was excited would be an understatement. Even when telling me about this after the fact, Samir could barely contain himself, he was so delighted. He could hardly get his mind around the fact that his failure had opened the door to such an amazing opportunity. While AI had yet to become a strategic priority or initiative, it was on the strategy roster, so when the time was right, the company would be ready to act.

When I say that culture influences and informs strategy, this is what I mean. The way both high-tech companies approached strategic planning and the strategies they adopted can be clearly linked to the beliefs of the company's leaders. These beliefs shaped the culture, which influenced the strategy. The lesson is twofold. First, if a company doesn't identify and address a strategy gap, this may be the result of the culture and the beliefs of the company's leaders. Second, leaders typically do not understand, because they don't think about it, how their beliefs influence their choices and decisions and thereby influence strategy. These biases are, for most of us, accepted truths that unconsciously shape our worldview and, therefore, our actions.

WHEN CULTURE IS THE PROBLEM

Regardless of their approach, not that long ago, many companies could go years, if not decades, without changing their strategy. Even if a significant event happened in the external environment, these companies remained relatively unaffected. Large telecommunications companies like AT&T and Bell Canada are just two examples. However, the world has changed, and stability is now a luxury for most companies. In this new world, it is the companies that respond quickly and effectively to external change that have a significant competitive advantage.

This is why understanding culture drag is so important. It isn't enough to recognize and take action to close a strategy gap; companies need to also change the culture, and quickly. If they don't, they risk a disconnect between strategy and culture, resulting in culture drag, which interferes with strategy execution, negatively impacting the company's performance and its ability to achieve its goals. In this way, the culture that contributed to past success becomes a serious business problem.

The first step in solving any problem is to understand what, precisely, the problem is. The model of culture-strategy alignment (diagram 5) provides a simple yet powerful tool to help leaders do exactly that. By working with the other leaders on your team to complete the model, you can achieve the shared understanding and commitment necessary to determine what changes are needed, if any. One option would be to adjust your strategy so it is consistent with your company's current culture. Instead of changing the culture, you can focus on how to modify your strategy to take advantage of its strengths. If this is not an option, the only reasonable alternative is to change the culture to support your strategy, which can be a daunting proposition.

As mentioned in previous chapters, the main reason culture change efforts fail to achieve their goals is because leaders delegate the responsibility to HR instead of actively owning the change effort. This is not because they don't think it is important, nor is it because they don't care. In my opinion, this happens because we, the culture experts, have been advocating the wrong approach. As Edgar Schein, a renowned professor at the MIT Sloan School of Management who is widely recognized for his groundbreaking work in the field of organizational culture, so eloquently stated, "Don't focus on culture because it can be a bottomless pit."[20]

We can't change culture by focusing on values, beliefs, and behaviors; we need to focus on the business problem caused by the culture. Values, beliefs, and behaviors are important, but we get to these by solving the business problem and, as part of this, asking, "What will we see people doing when the problem is solved?" By starting with a business problem that can only be solved by changing the culture, culture change is viewed as a critical business priority, elevating it to the same level of importance and urgency as other demands on leaders' time and attention. However, while leaders have many skills and abilities, culture change is rarely one of them. For leaders to effectively lead culture change, they need a straightforward, results-oriented approach they can trust to deliver the outcomes needed. The approach must leverage the skills leaders already have, thereby giving them the confidence that, with a little help, they have what it takes to succeed.

The good news is that there is a solution, which is the CASPE culture change process. CASPE is a five-step process for solving culture problems that I developed and have successfully used in organizations for the past several years. It was sparked by the insights I gained from working with senior leaders wrestling with complex business problems. It is the culmination of decades spent searching for the answer to one question: how can we achieve timely, meaningful, and sustainable culture change in organizations?

CHAPTER SIX

THE CASPE CULTURE CHANGE PROCESS

THE CORE PRINCIPLE THAT is the basis for the design of the CASPE culture change process, and the reason that it works, is to **focus leaders' attention and energy on solving a business problem, *not* on changing the company's culture**. This is also what makes the CASPE process different from other culture change approaches. By starting with a problem, changes are identified that initiate a shift in beliefs about the way things need to be done. The result is intention—a purposeful change in behaviors, practices, processes, and so on leading to meaningful and sustained culture change.

The good news is that leaders deal with business problems every day. It is a basic part of their job. They know how to solve problems, and chances are they are really good at it. With CASPE, they apply their highly developed problem-solving skills to solve a business problem that is caused by culture. At the same time, they change the culture and strengthen culture-strategy alignment. It is straightforward and efficient and delivers results, unlike most approaches to culture change.

WHAT IS THE CASPE CULTURE CHANGE PROCESS?

The CASPE culture change process has five phases that follow the same basic steps used in classic approaches to problem-solving. The main difference is the emphasis on behaviors and the

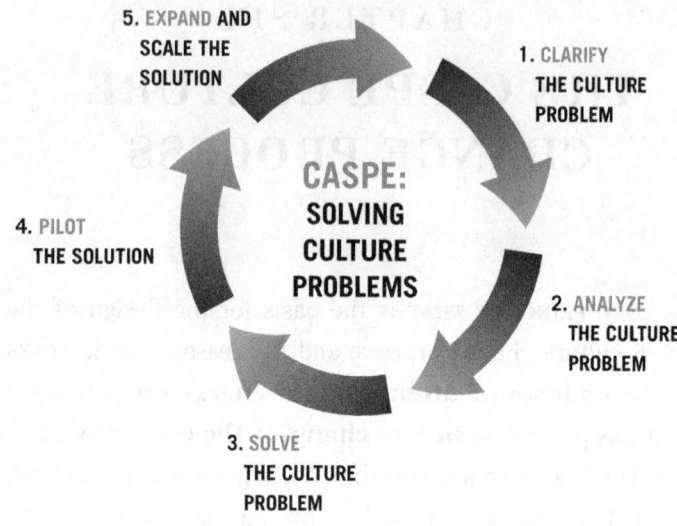

Diagram 6: The CASPE culture change process

changes in the environment required to encourage and sustain them. If you are thinking, *Hold on, this sounds like the culture change approaches that you said don't work,* relax. CASPE is different, and it is effective.

Most approaches to culture change focus on *what* needs to change (culture) versus *why* the change is needed (a business problem). For example, how do we create a more collaborative, innovative, or disciplined culture, or how do we create a culture of high engagement or trust? In contrast, CASPE emphasizes solving a business problem that is caused by culture. For example, why do we need to be more collaborative, innovative, or disciplined? What problem is this creating for the company? This is a very important difference, as the question that is asked determines what analysis takes place that leads to solutions and eventual action. If we ask the wrong question, we get the wrong answer. This is why the first phase of the CASPE culture change process stresses the importance of taking the time to achieve clarity and alignment before moving forward with analysis.

Phase One: Clarify the Culture Problem

Objective: Establish clarity and alignment with regard to the nature and importance of the business problem and agree that culture is a significant contributing factor

Participants: Leaders accountable for solving the business problem

Time Required: Two to three hours

Questions:
1. Why do we think we have a culture problem?
2. How is our culture causing or contributing to the business problem?
3. Where is the culture problem causing the most pain?

Overview:

The first phase of the CASPE culture change process is a two- to three-hour guided discussion conducted face-to-face, if possible. This is led by an expert facilitator certified in the CASPE process. The format itself is straightforward, consisting of three questions designed to clarify the problem and test for leader alignment. If these questions are answered, everyone should leave the meeting with a clear and shared understanding of why there is a culture problem, what the culture problem is, and where it is causing the most pain.

The first task in phase one is to check for alignment. While you may think everyone is on the same page and shares the same perspective, this is often not the case. Even if they are using the same words, their meaning and interpretation can be different.

With alignment confirmed, the next task is to identify specific pain points or situations where the culture is causing the business problem. As culture influences the way things get done in all parts of an organization, it should be easy to generate lots of examples. If, however, only one situation is identified, it is important to confirm that culture is the cause instead of something else. For example, a lack of collaboration can be caused by interpersonal conflicts within and between teams.

The next task is to select one situation from the list of pain points that urgently needs to be addressed. This makes the problem concrete and manageable. As Confucius once said, "The man who moves a mountain begins by carrying away small stones."[21] Attempting to solve a massive, organization-wide problem in one effort is never a good idea. It is too complex and requires too much time and too many resources and people, which can cause it to stall or get derailed. It is much more effective to identify specific pain points and attack each of these in a planful and coordinated manner.

Phase one concludes with a call to action to galvanize commitment and energy to engage in the culture change necessary to solve the problem. The culture-strategy alignment model is used to summarize the outcomes and provide a clear and memorable visual representation of how the current culture is interfering with strategy execution and why it needs to change to solve the business problem that can be referred to throughout the change effort.

Phase Two: Analyze the Culture Problem

Objective: Identify how the company's culture is causing the business problem

Participants: Leaders accountable for solving the business problem

Time Required: Three to four hours

Questions:

1. How are people currently behaving and working?
2. What will we see people doing and how will they behave when the problem is solved?
3. How do we make this happen?
4. What current situation can we use to test the solution?
5. What outcomes will be achieved when the culture problem is solved?

Overview:

Once a specific pain point is identified, the leaders dive deep into the situation to better understand how the current culture is contributing to the business problem. In this step, leaders describe the current situation in detail. The details are important, as they identify the behaviors that need to change and often provide insights into the belief system that drives behavior. This discussion of what is causing the current behavior can also provide valuable insights into how leaders are influencing people's behavior. This provides another checkpoint for testing whether leaders have bought into the need for change and, if they haven't, an opportunity to encourage them to critically reflect on how they might personally be contributing to the culture and the business problem. Reflection and self-awareness are essential for any culture change effort.

The next task is to focus on the future and identify what leaders will see when the problem is solved. What behaviors will we observe? What will the work environment be like? In effect, they describe the culture the organization needs to solve the business problem. Comparing the answers to the behaviors they are currently seeing makes the culture gap concrete. Next, the leaders identify ways to close the culture gap and solve the business problem by identifying changes that encourage people to demonstrate the desired behaviors. For example, if a lack of collaboration is negatively affecting innovation, an option might be to create integrated design teams consisting of people from different departments. To encourage collaboration, shared goals could be identified and used to measure individual and team performance, which would determine rewards.

The next task in phase two is to identify a specific occurrence of the problem to pilot the solution. The purpose of the pilot is to learn, identify obstacles and additional changes that are needed, and provide proof of concept. The pilot is determined by answering the following question: is there a specific situation that would provide a good test of the solution? A good test means that the pilot can be completed in a reasonable time frame, which is typically three to four months, and allows for a full test of the solution, not an incomplete or partial test.

Most organizations have multiple opportunities to test a solution. For example, research projects may be happening in several areas, such as artificial intelligence, robotics, virtual reality, and nanotechnology. Although each is relevant, it is important to select only one situation because of the work and time that is involved. The managers and employees participating in the pilot need to commit to a more rigorous approach to project management and a higher degree of transparency than normal. They may also have to learn new ways of working and behaving. The pilot also requires the active involvement of leaders, who observe the team, participate in team discussions, remove barriers, and provide formal and informal updates to senior leaders who are not directly involved in the pilot. It is unrealistic to expect that leaders will be able to dedicate the time this requires to more than one pilot.

Finally, the business and cultural outcomes and measurements used to evaluate success are identified. Keep in mind that it doesn't matter if behavior changes if this doesn't solve the business problem and produce the desired outcomes. Metrics are identified, and baseline performance measurements are established during the planning phase of the pilot and measured again upon its completion. Measurement of the culture change is important to prove how the change in culture was a factor in solving the business problem. This is essential to prove that the investment of time and resources is worthwhile, that changing the culture solves an important business problem, and that the CASPE culture change process works.

Phase Three: Solve the Culture Problem
Objective: Continue to build out the solution and identify the actions that need to be taken to implement the pilot

Participants: Leaders accountable for solving the business problem and managers responsible for implementing the pilot

Time Required: Three to four hours

Questions:

1. What are the strengths and weaknesses of this solution? What solution would be better?
2. How do we make this happen?
3. What would prevent behavior from changing?
4. What happens next?

Overview:

The solution identified in phase two is an important beginning; however, it is not the final answer. Although leaders have their perspectives, in most cases, they are too far removed from the day-to-day work to be aware of many of the factors that are contributing to the current situation. To make sure the solution is effective and can be implemented successfully, people who are close to the situation and know more about what is happening and why need to be engaged. This typically includes the managers responsible for doing the work. The managers' role is to validate and, if appropriate, identify a better solution and the specific actions required to implement it. They provide valuable insight into why things are done the way they are, as well as reveal other changes required to support new or different behaviors and ways of working. Engaging managers is also important for managing change. When managers believe that leaders have listened to their concerns and opinions and given serious consideration to their ideas and suggestions, they are more likely to advocate for the change.

This phase, however, is not just about employee communication, education, and engagement. Even more important is identifying what needs to happen to implement the pilot. For example, what needs to happen to strengthen collaboration in integrated design teams? Planning the pilot is similar to how you would approach any project or initiative. The main difference is the focus on behavior and, specifically, the changes in behavior needed to close the culture gap and solve the business problem.

The solution, if effective, should encourage and support these behaviors; however, behavior change is not easy for most of us. As we've discussed, our beliefs drive our behavior, and it takes time for these to shift. We also tend to get comfortable doing things a certain way and resist things that make us feel uneasy and uncomfortable. As a result, it is easy to hold on to old behaviors and ways of working, especially when things get tough and we're under pressure. If this happens, the culture gap won't be closed, and the problem won't be solved. The pilot will fail. This is one of the reasons it is important that leaders are actively involved in the pilot itself. While they may not directly participate in the work, they need to demonstrate, through their involvement, that holding on to the status quo is not an option. They do this by observing the team, participating in team meetings, holding people accountable for their behavior, and implementing the other changes needed for the pilot to be successful.

Lastly, the outcomes and metrics used to measure the pilot's success are finalized. Leaders identified these in phase two; however, the discussion that happens in phase three can result in changes to the selection or scope of the pilot. It is important that the measures used are perceived by managers to be realistic and achievable.

Phase 4: Pilot the Solution

Objective: To assess the feasibility and viability of applying the solution more broadly in the organization

Participants: Leaders accountable for solving the business problem and managers responsible for implementing the pilot

Time Required: Three to four months (maximum)

Questions:
1. What changes are needed to drive new behavior?
2. How are we doing (during pilot implementation)?
3. How did we do and what did we learn (after completion of the pilot)?

Overview:

This phase of the CASPE culture change process focuses on monitoring behavior change and capturing lessons learned, as well as measuring and reporting results. The pilot is a real work situation, not a special project, training program, or hypothetical scenario. It is work that needs to be done regardless of whether culture change is a part of it. As a result, managers and employees can easily get caught up in task completion. For this reason, it is important to be rigorous in planning and implementing an approach that monitors progress to identify, as early as possible, any adjustments or corrections needed to ensure a successful outcome. In some cases, monitoring is assigned to a project manager who is dedicated to the change effort. Alternatively, a member of the team or the manager could take on this responsibility. This also ensures that lessons learned during and at the end of the pilot are captured so they can be discussed and actioned.

Monitoring happens informally and formally throughout the pilot and at the end with a retrospective or postmortem. The informal monitoring is conducted by leaders who observe and interact with the team. Formal monitoring occurs in regular check-ins that piggyback on normal project meetings and are attended by the senior leaders accountable for the pilot. The discussion focuses on behavior, specifically whether the organization is seeing the behaviors that are needed to change the culture and solve the problem. If not, what is preventing behavior change? What changes are needed to correct this? The information gathered from these discussions is actioned, with the expectation that it will be addressed immediately. These interim check-ins also provide the leaders responsible for the change with information that can be used to communicate with other senior leaders and the rest of the organization. This should be interesting and relevant, linking the behavior change to work outcomes. In many cases, issues arise that are systemic in nature or outside of the pilot team's control to act on. Holding discussions on these issues with other senior leaders is an effective way to maintain interest and support and focus on the change effort.

The retrospective or postmortem that occurs at the conclusion of the pilot is a deep dive into the team's experience. In addition to evaluating the effectiveness of the change effort, it is used to generate lessons that can be applied to future initiatives. This includes identifying barriers that need to be addressed for culture change to be successful. For example, if integrated design teams are to be successful, the reward system may need to change to recognize team results versus individual and departmental results. This type of change has broader implications for the organization, and a decision requires the involvement of human resources and possibly finance. Another example would be if the pilot team determined that the current organization structure is a barrier and that reporting relationships need to change from departmental to project-based.

Ultimately, the pilot should prove that changing culture will solve the business problem. If it is determined that systemic and other barriers will limit the efficacy of the change effort, leaders will need to decide whether this is acceptable before moving forward with plans to expand the culture change effort to other parts of the company.

Phase Five: Expand and Scale
Objective: Develop a plan to apply the solution and lessons learned to accelerate culture change

Participants: Leaders accountable for solving the business problem

Time Required: Two to three hours

Questions:
1. How do we scale the solution to change the culture in other parts of the company?

Overview:
The outcomes of the pilot determine what happens next. If the pilot is successful, leaders are tasked with developing a plan to expand and scale the culture change in other parts of the company. If it isn't successful because of a lack of effective implementation or leadership, or because the barriers were too great to overcome, a decision needs to be made to either conduct a second pilot or abandon the effort.

Abandoning the effort is the right decision if it is determined that, despite indications to the contrary, leaders are unwilling or unable to take personal accountability or participate to the extent that is needed for the culture change to be successful. This discussion usually occurs between the facilitator, HR executive or team members, and the executive to whom the leaders report. As I have stated multiple times, without active leadership, culture change is doomed to fail. If this happens, leaders also need to accept that the probability that the business problem will be solved is low. If, on the other hand, the pilot failed to achieve its goals because the specific actions agreed on in step three were not implemented or the pilot team encountered obstacles they could not overcome, the better choice might be to select another occurrence of the problem and repeat the pilot. Of course, before doing so, it is important to address the obstacles encountered in the first pilot so the same problems aren't repeated.

If the pilot is successful and the decision is made to move forward and expand the culture change effort, the next task is to determine the scope of this phase. The best option is always to proceed in a planful and intentional manner that considers the organization's capacity and readiness for change and the potential return on investment. Occurrences or scenarios that are similar to the pilot are usually a good place to start, as you can apply the lessons learned. Repeating steps three and four of the CASPE process allows important differences in context to be identified and addressed. This also ensures that the employees affected by the change are engaged, thereby reducing the risk of resistance.

Another option for expanding the culture change effort is to repeat the CASPE culture change process starting at step one, revisiting the list of different problem scenarios leaders previously identified. Confirm or update the list and prioritize the scenarios based on their urgency and importance. Keep in mind that there are likely multiple incidences or occurrences of each scenario, then decide if you want to tackle all occurrences of a scenario at the same time or in stages. This decision depends on the leaders' and organization's capacity and capability to handle the change. Keep in mind that only the leaders involved in the pilot will have developed the competence to apply the CASPE process effectively. Ideally, these leaders will coach and support other leaders when they use CASPE for the first time. Until enough leaders have developed competence, expansion and scaling of the change will be limited. If the company can't afford to wait for this to happen, an option is to provide leaders with coaching and other support to accelerate the learning process.

In addition, attention can be directed to other examples of the current culture in action that, if addressed, would help the change effort gain traction. For example, we might see evidence of breakdowns in collaboration in the implementation of core business processes, sharing of information, coordination of new program implementation, and so on. The key is to determine where there is the greatest potential return on investment and tackle these challenges first.

APPLYING THE CASPE CULTURE CHANGE PROCESS

Hopefully, you now have a basic understanding of the CASPE process and want to learn more. In the following chapter, I share the story of one company's experience with CASPE, diving into more detail that provides insight into how it could be applied in your organization. One of the interesting aspects of this case is that I was initially approached by the CHRO to provide leadership coaching to one of the company's executives, not to help them change the culture. I mention this because it is not uncommon nor unusual for leaders to think they have a culture problem when it is something else altogether, and vice versa. This is why the first thing to do before initiating the CASPE process is to confirm there is a culture problem.

Sometimes, what appears to be a culture problem is a conflict between individuals and teams or can be attributed to the behavior of a specific person. To check for this, you need to determine if the situation or behavior that is problematic is consistent with the company's culture. If it is, then it should be easy to find other situations where the same or related behaviors are evident. If not, then it is likely not a culture problem but something else that requires a different approach, such as coaching or conflict mediation. That said, it is important to quickly address the situation, as failure to do so can result in either failed strategy execution or a toxic work environment that will negatively affect employee engagement, productivity, and performance. If, having given this some consideration, you believe your company has a culture problem, and you want to know how to solve it, then read on.

CHAPTER SEVEN

THE CASPE PROCESS
IN ACTION

A SEVENTY-FIVE-YEAR-OLD ENGINEERING AND manufacturing company—hereafter referred to as E&M—had a problem. Things had been going well until about three years ago when the company, which was a dominant player in the industry, began to lose an increasing number of competitive bids to provide its products and services to global and national customers. Initially, leaders thought this was simply a result of the normal competitive process and weren't worried. However, in the past twelve months, they had failed to win a single major bid. As a result, revenues were coming in well below target, and for the first time in decades, E&M was on track to report a year-over-year decline in profits. This was a crisis.

Upon investigation, E&M's executives learned their competitors were offering integrated solutions rather than the product-specific solutions E&M provided. This not only met the customers' requirements but did so at a substantially lower price. Furthermore, customers appreciated that the competitors provided them with a single point of contact for the bid response instead of having them interface with people from each product line, as was the case at E&M. It was abundantly clear that the only way E&M was going to be able to compete was for its three business units to work together and provide customers with integrated solutions. This would be a significant change from the way things had always been done. The business units were managed as independent entities, with their own profit and loss (P&L) statements and distinct portfolios of products and services. They were responsible for their own product development, manufacturing, marketing, installation, and customer service and were supported by centralized corporate functions such as finance and HR. The leaders of the business units were members of the executive team and met regularly to discuss strategy and other matters of concern to the company. Beyond this, there was very little interaction between them. They were heads down, running their businesses.

The CEO recognized the challenge and, as a result, met with the three business unit leaders separately and together to emphasize that they needed to find a way to integrate their products and services. He was also very clear that their goals and financial targets were not changing. This meant the business unit leaders, with the support of the corporate functions, needed to find a way to recoup lost revenues, which required closing deals. Despite this and similar subsequent conversations, one business unit refused to collaborate with the others and continued to operate independently. The leader of the business unit in question was an experienced executive—whom I will refer to as Caroline.

Both the CEO and CHRO spoke with Caroline about this, and her response was to ask if they trusted her to run her business. Of course, they said, "Yes," to which she replied that they needed to let her do so. While they had hoped she would be open to feedback, they weren't surprised by her stance. Caroline and the other business unit leaders had the accountability, authority, and autonomy to run their businesses as they saw fit so long as they delivered results. Until recently, Caroline's business unit had met or exceeded every financial target. She had an excellent personal track record of performance and had proven she could overcome any challenge thrown her way. Telling her what to do and how to do it would be unwarranted and met with extreme resistance.

The CHRO and the CEO were stumped, which led to the decision to reach out to me in the hope that I could coach Caroline and somehow convince her to change her behavior to be more collaborative. The CHRO acknowledged that this was a long shot, but they didn't know what else to do. They believed that, given enough time, she would eventually come around; however, the company couldn't afford to wait for this to happen. If things didn't change quickly, they would be forced to replace her. I asked the CHRO to bear with me, as I wanted to make sure I understood the situation. For the next thirty minutes, we talked about the company, its culture, and the changes that were needed. At the end of the conversation, I shared that it was interesting that the first thing she said to me was that Caroline was the problem. What I was hearing was that the culture was the problem. The need to provide customers with integrated solutions, not just an integrated response to a proposal, demanded behaviors and ways of working that were very different than those currently in practice. Solving the problem would take more than changing Caroline's behavior. I then explained the CASPE process and how it could help to solve their problem. If, during the process, Caroline thought it would be helpful to also receive coaching, then great. A few weeks later, we launched the CASPE culture change process at the company. Spoiler alert, it worked, and E&M won its first of many competitive bids for integrated solutions.

Lesson #23 — More often than not, it's what not who is the problem.

This is an important lesson. I often get approached to help organizations solve people problems when the real issue is the culture. This is not to say that people problems don't exist, because we all know that they do. Performance and behavior issues happen all the time. In Caroline's case, it would be easy to believe she was the problem. Her behavior was clearly interfering with the collaboration required for the business units to work together to provide customers with integrated solutions. The question was why? Why did she believe it was not just okay but best for her and her team to work independently?

Remember, it is always important to assume positive intent. Caroline was doing what she did because she believed it was the best and right thing for the company. This needed to be respected. Telling her that she was wrong and needed to change would be deeply insulting. Instead, the objective was to help her adjust her perspective to accommodate the realities of a changing marketplace. In my experience, if the leader is an executive, it is best for HR/OD to hire an experienced coach who has a deep understanding of culture and organizational dynamics for this work. An executive coach provides a neutral and objective perspective and is someone the executive can trust to protect confidences. Knowing the coach has their best interests at heart, the executive is usually more willing to be vulnerable and open up about their thoughts and experiences, engage in reflection, and consider alternative perspectives and paths forward. While it is possible for a senior HR/OD professional to assume this role, it is difficult for someone in the organization to duplicate these dynamics even if there is a good relationship with the executive.

CASPE PHASE ONE: CLARIFY THE CULTURE PROBLEM

The entire executive team was accountable for E&M's strategy and its performance. The problem the company faced affected both. If E&M decided to offer integrated solutions, it would have far-reaching implications, affecting the company's business model, brand, offers, structure, and so on. This impacted not only the business units but also the corporate functions that supported them. As an example, finance was involved in pricing, legal contributed to contracts and negotiations, and human resources provided guidance and support if the changes affected people. Every person on the executive team would be affected. As a result, the CEO and CHRO decided that the entire executive team would participate in the first phase of CASPE.

Once the decision was made to involve the entire executive team, a call was arranged so the CEO—whom we will call Michel—could introduce me to his team and I could provide an overview of the CASPE process. He explained that he would be actively involved in the entire process and that my role was to help facilitate and guide him and the team. The CHRO was a participant, just like the other executives. She was not leading this initiative, he was. He ended the meeting by noting the date and time of the first workshop and saying he expected everyone to attend, no exceptions.

As a side note, these decisions were made in a planning meeting I facilitated with the CEO, CHRO, and senior OD leader who partnered with me on the initiative. Prior to the meeting, I sent them an overview of the CASPE process and asked them to come prepared with questions. This allowed us to minimize the time required to explain the process so we could focus on the decisions needed to move forward with phase one. This included determining who would attend the phase one workshop, what actions should take place prior to the workshop, and timing. We also discussed the governance of the initiative, focusing on roles and responsibilities, status updates, broader communication, key success factors, and how success would be measured. An outcome of this meeting was the decision for me to conduct one-hour, one-on-one interviews with each of the executives to understand their perspectives of the problem (listen and learn), answer questions about the CASPE process (educate), and establish my credibility (build trust). These interviews are always valuable, as they often reveal differences in perspective that provide context that is important to know before entering workshop discussions. While the CEO asked if the CHRO or OD leader should also be on the calls, I recommended against this, as it would increase the risk that the culture change would be viewed as HR/OD's responsibility. As noted earlier in this book, this is something to be avoided at all costs.

The Phase One Workshop

The first phase of the CASPE process is a two- to three-hour guided discussion conducted face-to-face, if possible. In my experience, face-to-face discussions tend to generate more energy and debate than those held virtually. It also makes it easier to judge when someone is withholding their opinion or disagrees with a decision. While the sponsor can lead this workshop, in most cases, I find that they prefer to participate and ask me to facilitate. However, the more the sponsor is seen to be leading the process, the more likely it is to be given importance by others. For this reason, I encourage the sponsor to at least cofacilitate the discussion with me. As cofacilitators, we have distinct roles. Mine is to manage the process and discussion, making sure the objectives are met, while the sponsor's role is to ask questions that challenge people to broaden and deepen their thinking. If the CHRO attends, they are to participate, not lead, observe, or facilitate. They need to be seen as an active stakeholder, the same as every other participant. I do, however, encourage HR/OD professionals to be present for knowledge transfer and learning, with the intention that they can fill my role in applying the CASPE process going forward. We'll discuss this in more detail later in this book.

The format of the workshop itself is straightforward. The workshop is opened by the executive sponsor—in E&M's case, this was Michel—who reiterates why they are here (the business problem or situation facing the company) and what he expects not just for this workshop but for the entire initiative. It is important to point out that I coached Michel on what to say during his introduction to make sure he provided sufficient context and a sense of urgency while not offering solutions. This included not stating his view of the culture problem, as this could influence what the other people in the room would say, which would be detrimental to achieving the desired outcomes. This is something I strongly recommend going into every workshop.

The sponsor's kickoff is followed by a recap of the CASPE process using insights and examples drawn from my interview notes. This includes a brief question-and-answer session, after which the focus shifts to the rest of the agenda. This consists of three questions designed to clarify the problem and test for leader alignment. If these questions are answered, everyone should leave the meeting with a clear and shared understanding of why there is a culture problem, what the culture problem is, and where it is causing the most pain.

Question #1—Why do we think we have a culture problem?

In his introduction, Michel reminded his executive team that the business problem was the company's failure to win a single competitive bid for national and global customers' business in the previous twelve months. There was also no evidence this would change unless they did things differently. He reviewed the results of the investigation regarding the cause and, in a strongly worded statement, told the team they needed to find a solution. With this expectation established, he asked the team how they thought the current culture was contributing to the problem. This is another way of wording the first question that works well if you are starting with a business problem. If leaders are aligned in the belief the company has a culture problem, then asking why they think they have a culture problem works well.

The answers from E&M's leaders consisted mostly of broad references such as how a lack of collaboration was negatively affecting operational efficiency and how a lack of clear goals and strategy was making it difficult to set priorities. One business leader pointed to the need for greater integration of products and services but didn't mention anything about the culture. A couple of executives even stated they didn't think the company had a culture problem. Eventually, after much discussion and some pointed questions from Michel, the leaders agreed that the company's siloed culture was a factor and that this had to change if E&M was to offer solutions that integrated products and services from the three business units. This was followed by a lengthy discussion of what they meant by "siloed culture," during which the leaders shared example after example of how this was evident every day in various aspects of the business. They also discussed how the shift to integrated solutions had wide-ranging implications, as it affected almost every aspect of the business. For example, product development was currently isolated within product lines. This would need to change so that it was integrated across multiple product lines. Similarly, customer-facing processes, including sales, installation, and service, would need to be reengineered. The list went on and on. The bottom line was that the company's siloed culture was an obstacle to developing integrated product solutions for its customers.

Question #2—How is our culture causing or contributing to the business problem?

When asked to explain how the siloed culture prevented E&M from providing customers with integrated solutions, the leaders described how each business unit operated autonomously. People's career paths were restricted to their business unit, so they had little knowledge of the other businesses, which meant they didn't understand when something they heard or were working on would be of value to the other teams. All product development happened within the business unit, so new knowledge and ideas that could benefit other business units were rarely shared. Marketing was also specific to the business unit, with each having its own brand and strategy. They never piggybacked on one another's efforts to gain exposure with new customers or in new markets. Another executive explained how two business units competed for the same customers' business, forcing the other to lower its price. As for submitting a bid that required products and services from two or more business units, currently, each wrote their part of the proposal separately and someone pulled it together. This was an independent exercise in keeping with the siloed culture.

Question #3 — Where is the culture problem causing the most pain?

In E&M's case, there was an obvious choice. The most pressing need was to win competitive bids for national and global customers' business. To accomplish this, the company needed to offer an integrated, price-competitive solution in response to customer requests for proposals (RFPs). The lack of collaboration between the three business units meant that all aspects of the company's responses to RFPs were disjointed. The submission was fragmented, the solution was messy and overly complex, the price was too high, and there were too many points of contact for the customer. Unless the business units broke down the siloes and started to work together, the problem the business faced was not going away.

Question #4 — A call to action

The workshop wrapped up with an activity designed to galvanize commitment and energy to engage in the culture change necessary to solve the problem. The activity was led by Michel, with my assistance. The activity asked the team to complete the culture-strategy alignment model (see chapter five) as a summary of the discussion and to confirm alignment and commitment. At E&M, this was done in a full group; however, in other organizations, I have asked participants to complete the exercise individually and share their results. This is an effective way to check for alignment and address discrepancies. This exercise can also be done in pairs, triads, or small teams.

With the model complete, Michel checked that the leaders agreed it was an accurate summary of the discussion and were committed to the solution identified to close the strategy and culture gaps. He made it very clear there was no going back. If

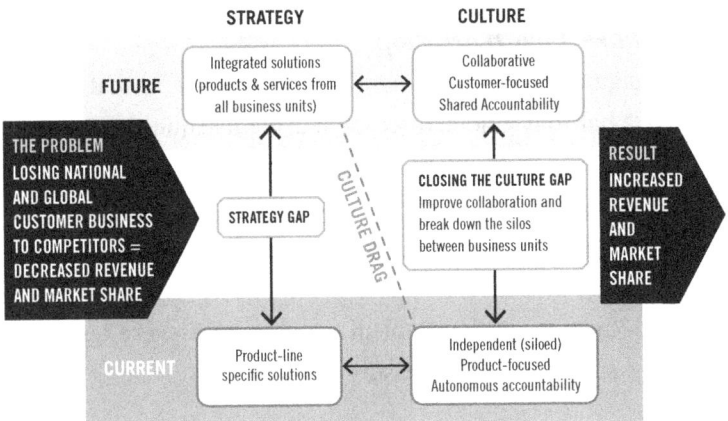

Diagram 7: Culture-strategy alignment at E&M

anyone had concerns, this was the time to voice them. When the meeting ended, he expected everyone to be aligned and committed to the change effort. Finally, he set the stage for phase two, explaining that the objective was to thoroughly understand the culture gap—how we do things now versus how we need to do things to solve the business problem.

CASPE PHASE TWO: ANALYZE THE CULTURE PROBLEM

The primary objective of phase two is to identify the changes in behavior required to solve the specific problem identified as a pain point in phase one. This involves conducting a deep dive into the culture gap to understand what behaviors currently exist and compare them to the behaviors needed to solve the problem. As was the case with E&M, some companies decide to complete phases one and two in a single session. The obvious benefit is continuity, which saves time, as there is no need to re-establish context or review the outcomes or decisions. There is also the advantage of reduced costs and fewer logistics to manage, especially if people are traveling from different locations.

The Phase Two Workshop

The design of phase two is similar to phase one in that it consists of a half-day guided discussion using five questions and is conducted face-to-face when possible. The sponsor, facilitator, and HR/OD roles are also the same. The first three questions focus on the changes to behaviors that are needed to solve the problem and how to make this happen. The last two identify an active occurrence of the problem situation to use as a test case and how success is to be measured.

Question #1—How are people currently behaving and working?

This question is used to describe the way work is currently being done. The objective is to gather enough information to have a comprehensive and accurate understanding of the situation. Anchoring the discussion with the specific problem scenario or pain point provides focus and prevents the conversation from getting bogged down in abstract concepts and what-if scenarios. At E&M, the problem scenario or pain point the executive team selected was to win competitive bids for national and global customers' business by offering integrated, price-competitive solutions in response to requests for proposals.

In answering the question, the leaders described that when a customer RFP was received, it was divvied up to the sales teams in the three business units based on the required products and services. The sales teams would then prepare their part of the proposal. The business unit with the largest piece of the proposal assigned a coordinator, who was responsible for combining everything into one document and checking that it met the RFP submission requirements. The compiled proposal was then sent to the business unit executives for final approval.

If there were concerns or issues with the submission, the executives involved would attempt to reach a resolution. Most issues were resolved in this manner; however, pricing was consistently an obstacle, as the business unit leaders were unwilling to do anything that would negatively impact their ability to achieve their business unit's revenue targets. This resulted in impasses and most proposals being submitted with the original pricing.

As noted, all work required to complete the proposal and review process was conducted independently. For example, members of each business unit's sales team attended customer information meetings and proposal presentations. They would also bring their own technical experts, who sometimes provided conflicting information. If the sales teams had questions about the RFP, they submitted them to the customer separately and didn't share the questions or answers with the other business units' teams. As a result, they sometimes asked the same questions, which customers found a frustrating waste of time. In addition, each sales team provided the customer with a list of business unit contacts to reach out to if they had questions or required further information. The feedback from customers was that this was also frustrating, as it meant they frequently had to make multiple calls to get answers to their questions.

At no point during the process did the sales teams exchange information or work together, and there was absolutely no communication between product development, installation, service, or other teams. In fact, stories were told of sales teams withholding information that could have helped another business unit with their part of the proposal. To reiterate, everything was done separately. As a result, the proposed solution, and the proposal itself, was disjointed, the price was not competitive, and potential customers were frustrated.

Question #2—What will we see people doing and how will they behave when the problem is solved?

This question shifts the focus to the future to identify what you will see people doing when the problem is solved. Think of this as a visioning and brainstorming exercise. If all is right with the world, the problem is solved, and you are winning competitive bids for integrated solutions, how are people behaving and what are they doing? How are they working together?

Michel decided to be direct in his approach to this question. To him, the answer was obvious, and he said as much to the leaders. The sales teams needed to work together on the entire end-to-end RFP process. He asked if anyone disagreed, which was met with silence. He then asked, "So what does this look like?" The E&M leaders began describing behaviors they would see if this was happening. For example, the sales teams would work together to develop a plan for the proposal process that included identifying roles and responsibilities, timelines, and deliverables. They would meet regularly to discuss their progress, identify issues, and decide on actions to be taken. They would coordinate their questions for the customer so they weren't repeated, would share the answers with the other teams, and so on.

Question #3—How do we make this happen?

The third question asks the leaders to identify the changes required to encourage and sustain the behaviors identified in question two. If anyone says, "We'll just tell people that this is what they need to do and how they are expected to behave," ask them how well that has worked so far. The answer is it hasn't.

E&M's leaders decided that, for people to behave in a way that solved the problem, they had to break down the siloes.

They couldn't have the sales teams continuing to work independently and expect that simply insisting on more communication and better coordination would change anything. They needed to do something dramatic. Their solution was to create integrated teams consisting of people from the three business units who would be responsible for the customer RFP process. The teams would include people from sales, support, and technical areas as needed and be led by a team leader agreed on by the business unit leaders. The business unit leaders would continue to approve the submissions but would review the entire document instead of only their part. If issues arose that required an executive decision, the business unit leaders would work together to resolve them.

Several obstacles and potential barriers were also identified and discussed, such as the fact that reporting relationships, performance appraisals, and rewards were business-unit-centric. The leaders decided that the most pressing concern was how performance would be assessed and rewards, especially year-end bonuses, determined. While this had broader implications for the organization that meant it would normally be out of scope, they believed that failure to act on this topic could derail the change effort. As a result, the decision was made for HR to develop a temporary solution that would be reevaluated after the pilot was completed. The issue with reporting relationships was "parked," as they decided this was not as urgent.

Finally, the leaders discussed limitations and constraints of the solution. For example, they agreed the new integrated teams would be staffed by existing employees and funded by the business units. There wasn't going to be additional hiring or money allocated to the initiative. It was important to identify this at this stage, as the next phase of the CASPE process expands participation to include lower-level managers. If there are limitations, these need to be clearly communicated.

Question #4—What current situation can we use to test or pilot the solution?

Most organizations have multiple occurrences of the problem scenario happening at any given time. At E&M, the business units' sales teams were preparing bid submissions for integrated solutions in response to three active national and global customer RFPs. While it is tempting to tackle every occurrence, this makes the initiative significantly more complex and challenging and decreases the probability of achieving a successful outcome. Instead, select one specific occurrence of the problem to be the test case. When selecting the test case, it is important to first identify the selection criteria. This usually includes the likelihood of success and the ability to complete the test in three to four months. In addition, the test case, or pilot, should allow for a full test of the solution, not an incomplete or partial test.

At E&M, success was defined by winning a competitive bid for an integrated solution in the next three months. Of the three submissions that were active, one was in the final stages of preparation, and the second was almost entirely limited to one business unit with minor additions from a second business unit. The third, however, involved an RFP that had only recently been received by the company and was large enough in scope to require the involvement of all business units. It was an obvious choice to select this third option as the pilot.

Question #5—What business outcomes will we see when the culture problem is solved?

The objective of the fifth and final question in phase two is to identify the outcomes and measurements used to evaluate success. This is essential to prove that the investment of time and resources is worthwhile, that changing the culture solves an important business problem, and that the CASPE process works. There are two aspects to this. The first and most important is the business outcomes and measures that are specific to the test case or pilot. The second is the culture outcomes and measures that are more broadly applicable.

At E&M, the executive team identified one business outcome. This was to close the deal with the customer and generate $3.4 million in revenue for the company. Note that, for the first time, the revenue target was for the company, not the business units. This was intentional to encourage those involved to make pricing and other decisions that were in the best interests of the company, even if it meant the business unit had to take a hit. The culture outcome and measurement they chose was feedback from the customer indicating the team and company were easy to work with. Drawing on prior customer feedback, they defined "easy to work with" as the proposal seamlessly integrating the company's portfolio of products and services, a single point of contact for customer questions, and so on. They believed the only way the team could achieve this was to demonstrate the collaborative behaviors the leaders had identified. If this happened, it would be a good indicator that the culture had changed, at least within this team. With the culture problem defined, the behaviors identified, and a potential solution and pilot determined, E&M was ready to embark on phase three of the CASPE process.

CASPE PHASE THREE: SOLVE THE CULTURE PROBLEM

In phase three, senior leaders continue to actively participate in the change effort; however, participation is widened to include the managers who are responsible for the work. The managers' role is to validate the solution identified by the senior leaders in phase two and determine the specific actions required to implement it. These discussions provide insights into why things are done the way they are, as well as reveal changes required to support new or different behaviors and ways of working. By actively participating, senior leaders also demonstrate they are committed to making the changes necessary to solve the problem.

Engaging managers also provides an opportunity for communication and education. As with any major change, it is important to explain why the change is needed and allow people to ask questions. This helps to ensure that the managers have an accurate and comprehensive understanding of the problem and the proposed solution. When they believe that senior leaders have listened carefully to their concerns and opinions and given serious consideration to their ideas and suggestions, they are more likely to accept instead of resist the change. In addition, when managers are engaged in developing solutions that are then implemented, they are more likely to advocate for the change, which is a powerful way to expand employee buy-in and commitment. This phase, however, is not just about communication, education, and engagement. Just as important is the task of identifying what needs to happen to implement the solution.

The Phase Three Workshop

While it is important for senior leaders to demonstrate ownership, accountability, and commitment to the change effort,

E&M rightly decided it would be overwhelming, and unproductive, for the entire executive team to participate in this workshop. Instead, they decided that Michel, as the sponsor, and the business unit leaders who were accountable for the pilot would represent the executive team. They also decided the business unit leaders would take a more active role in this workshop. As the CASPE expert, I would facilitate, while Michel would observe and step in when he felt it important to emphasize a point or make a course correction. By having the business unit leaders more actively involved, it was believed the managers would decide to do the same.

Phase three is a half-day working session that is part communication and engagement and part problem-solving and action planning. The main objective is to continue to build out the solution and identify the actions that need to be taken to implement the pilot. However, before this can happen, we need to bring the new team members, the managers, up to speed. The approach taken will be dictated by your company's culture. E&M's culture, in addition to being siloed, was very results-, goal-, and task-oriented. In keeping with this, Michel and the business unit leaders chose to provide an overview of the CASPE process and walk the managers through the completed culture-strategy alignment model, explaining how the executive team arrived at their conclusions. They then showed the managers how they had defined the culture gap (current versus future behavior) and the solution they believed would close the gap, which was to create an integrated sales/support team. Throughout, managers were invited to ask questions and challenge the leaders' conclusions.

Question #1 — What are the strengths and weaknesses of this solution? What solution would be better?

While the solution the senior leaders identify might be the best option, this isn't necessarily the case. The purpose of these questions is to identify the best solution to the problem. The managers are the people accountable for managing the day-to-day activities where behaviors are put into practice. Their buy-in and support of the change are essential. They also understand why things are done the way they are and what will prevent people from changing their behavior. As a result, they can provide constructive feedback as well as alternatives and suggestions.

In E&M's case, the managers were excited by the opportunity to work as an integrated team, sharing how frustrated they were with the current way of doing things. They quickly validated the solution proposed by senior leaders and immediately began asking questions about how this would work, which provided a great segue for the business unit leaders to say that this was where they needed the managers' help.

Question #2 — How do we make this happen?

The team was broken into smaller groups and asked to brainstorm everything they believed needed to happen for the pilot to be successful. The only caveat was that they were to identify actions, not questions. Initially, the managers didn't trust this instruction and asked questions such as, "Who is going to decide who is on the team?" to which the business unit leaders replied, "You tell us." It only took a few such examples for the managers to believe the executives were serious and shift into problem-solving mode.

They quickly began to identify tactical changes, including the composition of the team, which they recommended be expanded to include a finance person to help with the cost estimate, engineers to provide technical advice, and a project manager to prepare a plan and track progress. They also identified the need to colocate team members in the same physical space and provide them with access to customer data currently restricted to business unit employees. Other ideas included implementing agile development practices such as sprints, stand-up meetings, and Kanban boards, as well as a structured approach to provide updates to senior managers. The list was extensive.

Once all the ideas were noted, a business unit leader explained the constraints, which immediately eliminated the idea to rent an office space to colocate the team. This would require additional funds that were not available. The managers critically evaluated the remainder of the ideas and prioritized them to arrive at a final set of actions they believed would have the most impact and could be realistically implemented during a three- to four-month pilot. Almost every idea met these criteria; however, some were more difficult or complicated to implement, such as the suggestion to adopt agile development practices. While the managers felt this could be helpful, they acknowledged it would require time and training that could be distracting.

Question #3 — What would stop behavior from changing?

For the pilot to achieve its objectives, the integrated team would need to operate differently from the rest of E&M. The managers and other employees would need to work collaboratively to build a fully integrated and effective solution and offer it at a competitive price if they were to close the deal for the national customer's business. While they had identified the actions needed to support the team, there was a risk that the bigger entity, the company and its culture, would unknowingly sabotage the team's efforts.

An example of this provided by one of the business unit leaders was the current practice of restricting access to customer information to business unit employees. The team could probably work around this, but a more efficient solution would be to build one system that integrated the data from the three business units. The problem was that this would be expensive and take too long to accomplish for the pilot. A second but workable solution was to allow team members access to the business unit databases. He also explained that the executive team recognized that they needed to adjust how performance was appraised and rewards were determined. He then asked the managers what other obstacles they should be aware of.

As a facilitator, I am alert to cues that can provide insights into the company's culture. It was interesting to watch the nonverbal communication among the managers. It was obvious from the side glances and body movements that the business unit leader had hit on a couple of elephants in the room the managers were reluctant to mention. In doing so, he and the other leaders gained credibility, and the managers became more forthcoming. Among the obstacles and concerns they identified, several were directly related to the behavior and actions of more senior leaders, including the business unit executives. For example, if a leader pulled team members away to work on other business unit initiatives, even if they replaced them with another person, this would be highly disruptive. Others included senior leaders pressuring team members to advocate for including their business unit's products when they weren't needed and being unwilling to compromise on pricing. They also talked about potential problems with decision-making, given that the leaders of the three business units had to reach an agreement on the bid submission. What went unsaid was that this was what was happening now. The managers were skeptical that anything would change, and for good reason. Other potential problems included a lack of support and responsiveness from the corporate functions and difficulties working as a team when members barely knew one another or the other businesses.

As the team noted their concerns, the leaders listened and asked clarifying questions. Eventually, when the discussion ebbed, a business unit leader asked if there was anything else they needed for the integrated team to be successful. Then, in front of all the managers, Michel and the business unit leaders discussed what they had heard and identified the actions they would take. These were documented to be used as reference if the managers' concerns surfaced during the pilot. Finally, the discussion shifted to the next steps for moving forward with the pilot.

Question #4—What happens next?

Prior to the session, the business unit leaders had met to identify who from their teams would be assigned to the pilot. This list was presented to the managers, who suggested a few changes, such as adding a project manager from the PMO and assigning a financial analyst. They then discussed high-level roles, responsibilities, and reporting relationships. Finally, they agreed to convene a meeting of the business unit leaders and managers to work through the RFP process and identify the changes needed to drive collaborative behavior.

CASPE PHASE FOUR: PILOT THE SOLUTION

Phase four is challenging, as it typically requires that people step out of their comfort zone and do things differently than they have in the past. While this is difficult at the best of times, if the work involved is time-sensitive and the stakes are high, it creates added stress and pressure that can cause people to fall back into old behavior. There are three strategies built into phase four to prevent this from happening.

The first is to identify and implement the change in stages that mirror the work process. Stage one is the planning phase, when the team identifies the changes required to get started. The final stage is when the pilot concludes and changes are identified for future initiatives. In between are stages that mirror the steps in the work process. The number varies based on the process; however, at a minimum, there is one review and planning session to assess progress, adjust, and identify any further changes needed. Senior leaders participate in these sessions.

The second strategy is for leaders to monitor the change, especially behavior, by informally observing, asking questions, and interacting with the team. This provides firsthand information that can be used to detect issues and act on them. This is especially important in the early stages of the pilot, as this is when people usually question how committed senior leaders and the company are to the change. By observing and catching people demonstrating the right and wrong behaviors, leaders quickly and effectively make it clear that they are serious.

The third strategy is to build in check-ins throughout the implementation phase. These follow the same format, which makes it easy for the team to remember and apply them. These are in addition to the planning sessions and typically piggyback on other regularly scheduled team meetings. The purpose is to drive accountability for change by explicitly talking about behavior. Where are we making progress, where do old behaviors still exist, and what is stopping us from changing our behavior? The check-ins are driven by the team, and senior leaders are encouraged to attend. The more visible and active senior leaders are in the change process, the more likely people are to change their behavior.

You may be wondering how HR/OD is involved. As culture experts or experts in training, we view what happens through a unique lens. We see things that most leaders don't simply because this is what we are trained to do. As such, our role is to observe and share what we learn with the business unit leaders and managers when this adds value to their efforts. This is not an academic exercise. The purpose is to facilitate culture change by identifying signs that progress is being made as well as when it is not and why this might be the case. With this insight, we can work with the leaders and managers to make the necessary course corrections to increase the likelihood the culture change and pilot are successful.

Question #1—What changes are needed to drive new behavior?

At E&M, as should be the case for every organization that uses the CASPE process, the pilot was an active, time-sensitive work initiative. There wasn't the luxury of a long planning or training period. This made the E&M pilot challenging and created greater risk; however, it had the advantage of being mission-critical, which generated the attention of executives and other senior leaders.

As E&M had a clearly defined process for responding to customer RFPs, the managers and business unit leaders used this to identify the changes needed to drive the new behavior. Basically, the steps and tasks identified in the process did not change. For example, questions about the RFP were prepared and sent to the customer; however, how the team did this needed to be different. Instead of each business unit's sales team preparing and sending in separate lists, there was to be one combined list sent from one person on the integrated team. A lot of questions arose during this exercise, many about details such as whether the sales teams should prepare separate lists and then have someone compile them into a single document or if the sales teams should work on the list together. This exercise was critical, as it made things real. The managers and business unit leaders, by wrestling with the question of how to operate as an integrated team, began to understand the extent of the change that was needed.

They recognized that it was important for everyone to be on the same page but that it was even more important for employees to be part of the conversation. They would be doing most of the work, and they needed to understand what things were changing and why. While the management team needed to be aligned on major items, they decided it would be better to hold a separate meeting with the full pilot team to work through the details. Michel, upon hearing this plan, asked to be included in the meeting. Although the meeting was led by the business unit leaders, simply by being present, Michel made it clear this was an important initiative that he and the company were monitoring closely.

The meeting with employees began with an overview of the situation, using the culture-strategy alignment model to explain why change was needed. Once the context was established, the discussion shifted to how to make this happen. How was the team going to work together to win the bid for an integrated solution? They then pulled up the RFP process and, starting with the first phase, discussed how each task was to be completed. The changes identified were extensive, and you could see the team starting to become overwhelmed. This is one reason to not try to tackle the entire process in one sitting.

Question #2—How are we doing?
In keeping with the CASPE process, Michel and the business unit leaders committed to check in informally and observe the team in action. Given the demands on their time, this was challenging, especially because the team wasn't colocated. In fact, they quickly realized this was a distinct disadvantage and potentially a game changer, as the team struggled to collaborate. As a result, the decision was made early in the pilot to rent an office space in a nearby building. This made an immediate difference and, again, emphasized to the team that senior leaders, including the CEO, were committed to the change. This was just one example. By observing the team in action, Michel and the business unit leaders were able to identify obstacles and remove them before they caused a significant problem. This is not to say everything went smoothly; however, it did make things better.

The biggest challenge they encountered was, as anticipated, with pricing. While the team, and the business unit leaders, were able to put aside their business units' interests in designing a solution they felt was superior to what the competition could provide, they struggled to come to an agreement on the cost of the solution. The issue was that, to win the bid, the team felt they needed to offer products provided by one of the business units at a significantly discounted cost than the pricing sheet. Basically, Caroline, the business unit leader, was asked to take one for the team and make a decision that would negatively impact their revenue to do what was best for the company.

The problem was that if she agreed, her team would likely not meet the targets required to receive their year-end bonus. In other words, they would be punished for doing the right thing. This was exactly the issue that had been identified in phase two and that HR was supposed to help resolve. The problem was that this hadn't happened. Although HR had proposed a solution, Michel had not approved it. He felt the business units needed to hit their targets *and* do what was best for the company. In the end, the pricing issue was escalated to Michel, who made the decision. It did, however, create problems, especially later, when the other business units' team members received their bonuses and Caroline's team did not. This highlighted the fact that if the company planned to roll the solution out more broadly, this reward system would have to be addressed.

In addition to observing and interacting with the team, Michel and the business unit leaders made a point of attending the review and planning sessions the teams held at the end of each phase of the RFP process. They listened and asked questions, inserting their own observations and suggestions on occasion. They also made sure the discussion focused on behavior, not just tasks, which was what started to happen in the first meeting. They also participated in the final retrospective or review that was held at the conclusion of the pilot. All of this was in addition to normal activities conducted as part of the RFP process. In discussing their experience after the fact, they acknowledged they had significantly underestimated the time this would take, but they recognized it was important.

Question #3—How did we do?

Ultimately, the success of the pilot is measured by the results that are achieved, which in E&M's case was closing the deal to provide the national customer with an integrated solution and generating $3.4 million for the company. Arguably, this is all that is needed. The pilot achieved its objective of solving the business problem. However, it would be easy to lose sight of the fact that the reason this was possible was that the behavior of the people involved had changed. If there is interest in or intent of applying the solution or the CASPE process more broadly, it is important to show how changing behavior impacted the outcome. E&M accomplished this by having Michel contact the customer to ask about his experience. The customer shared that he was impressed with the changes E&M had made. They were much easier to do business with, which was in stark contrast to his prior experiences.

Michel shared what he'd heard with the team, the business unit leaders, and the rest of the executive team at the final retrospective, which was also a celebration. They talked about what people were doing differently, what had helped them to succeed, what obstacles they had to overcome, what they learned from the experience, the advice they had for other teams trying to do something similar, and what was needed to improve the experience. Obviously, it was too early to say that E&M's culture had changed; however, this was a significant step toward the collaborative way of working the company needed to execute its strategy.

CASPE PHASE FIVE: EXPAND AND SCALE THE SOLUTION

For E&M to change its culture from siloed to collaborative, there was a lot more work to be done. The pilot was only the beginning—a good one, but just a first step. It provided evidence that culture change was possible even in a seventy-five-year-old company that was set in its ways. It also proved that changing the culture, even in a small part of the organization, could solve an important business problem. The question was what to do next.

From personal experience and what they'd heard during the retrospective, Michel and the business unit leaders realized that scaling the change would be challenging. Beyond the effort required by the managers and teams doing the work, they had heard how important it was for senior leaders to be visible and involved throughout the pilot. Yet, maintaining this would be impossible if the company took on too much too fast. Scaling needed to be approached in a planful and intentional manner so that change was achieved without causing disruption to the business. At this point, my HR/OD partner took a more active role and worked with the leaders to address this need. I continued to be involved, but in more of an advisory capacity.

Question #1—How do we scale the solution to change the culture in other parts of the company?

Ultimately, E&M's leaders decided on a multipronged approach. The first decision was to apply the solution to other RFP responses by staffing these teams with members from the pilot team. In this way, they could leverage the pilot team's knowledge and experience to accelerate the change effort, and the members would model the behaviors for other teams. They also decided that a business unit leader would sponsor the change effort in each team, ensuring there was no question as to the commitment of the company and its leaders. This is an example of a wave strategy, meaning the change is rolled out in logical stages based on the organization's priorities, capacity, and capability. By starting with situations similar to the pilot, E&M could capitalize on the learning from this experience to streamline the approach. It also allowed them to skip phases one and two and go right to phase three, which saved time and money. In addition, they addressed the most significant pain point caused by a lack of collaboration, which was product integration across product lines. As success built, more evidence was collected to provide proof that culture change was possible and, furthermore, an essential competency that every leader needed to develop. Ultimately, the wave strategy creates a pull effect, meaning leaders start asking to learn how they can use the CASPE process to solve culture problems in their functions, departments, and teams.

This is also a good example of the amplifying effect that results when two or more leaders focus their energy and attention on solving the same culture problem, which in this case was breaking down the silos to create integrated sales teams. Because the leaders involved had participated in phases one and two of the CASPE process, they understood and supported the actions and decisions that had been made, including the behaviors that needed to change. As a result, even though they concentrated their efforts on different teams, their actions and messages were similar. In addition, practices were put in place to ensure the sponsors connected when anything happened that could benefit another team. This could be a new or unexpected challenge, such as the emergence of a new competitor or a request for a product not currently in the company's portfolio. However, it also included challenges with changing behavior and overcoming systemic barriers. This strengthened communication and relationships while modeling collaboration for the teams and other employees.

The second decision was to embark on a major change management initiative led by HR/OD that included employee communication, education, and engagement. The objective was to build broader awareness and understanding as well as managers' skills in creating and managing effective cross-functional teams, leading change, and using the CASPE process.

The third was to prioritize and act on several systemic barriers that had been identified, beginning with goal setting and total rewards. There was also discussion of reviewing the organization's structure and decision-making process, which was currently siloed. HR policies were also discussed, including building assessments of team skills into hiring practices and adding collaboration to performance assessments, at which point Michel told the other executives that he would be including this in his review of their performance starting immediately. To maintain focus and momentum, culture change was also added to the agenda of the executive team's monthly meetings and made a focus of upcoming strategy discussions.

IN CONCLUSION

E&M's experience is a good example of the CASPE culture change process in action in a large and complex organization. That said, the CASPE process also works to solve culture problems within and between departments and in small organizations. For example, a financial services company used it to improve the service its agents were providing to customers.

Another company applied it to solve a problem with new product development cycle times, while a third used it to address a quality problem in one of its production lines. What makes the CASPE process work is the focus on solving a business problem by changing behavior. It is straightforward and effective, but it is also intense. To be successful, it requires the commitment and active participation of senior leaders. Ultimately, this is the main deciding factor in determining if you are ready to use it in your organization.

Culture Change Begins with Leaders

As I have stated on numerous occasions, culture change only happens when leaders own and actively participate in the change effort, period. But what does it mean for leaders to "own" culture change?

Owning culture change starts with trusting the CASPE process and making the commitment to follow it as it was designed. This means not taking shortcuts, skipping steps, or avoiding questions that are tough or uncomfortable. It also means the leader is involved in every step. There is no handing it off to HR or delegating it to lower-level managers. During the pilot, the leader is fully present, observing and talking to team members, participating in team meetings, monitoring progress, and helping to address issues and remove barriers. The leader partners with HR/OD to manage the people side of change and share relevant information with other leaders and people who may not have visibility of the change, keeping them apprised of what is happening and the implications.

At the same time, the leader leads by example, meaning that if behaviors need to change, the leader is the first person to do so. If policies, processes, or structures need to change, the leader is the one who makes it happen. In other words, there is absolutely no doubt in anyone's mind that the leader is serious about changing the culture. All they have to do is listen to what the leader says and watch what the leader does to know that they are 100 percent committed to changing the culture. Unfortunately, this is not always the case. What to do when this happens is the focus of the next chapter.

CHAPTER EIGHT

LEADING THE WAY

THROUGHOUT THIS BOOK, I have repeatedly stated that the success of any culture change initiative, including CASPE, is determined in large part by the actions of leaders. To recap, what a leader says and does shapes the culture within their team and, depending on their influence, the entire organization. People constantly watch what leaders are doing for cues as to the expected way to behave and do things. This is why leaders' actions are more important than their words. If this consistency is lacking, the leaders send mixed messages that raise questions regarding what is really expected. As a result, most people take a wait-and-see position and default to existing behaviors and ways of doing things. The bottom line is that if people aren't changing their behavior, look no further than the leader to see why.

While many of the leaders I have worked with have the best of intentions and are self-aware, they often don't realize the extent to which their behaviors and actions influence others and shape the culture. This is where, as an HR/OD professional, you play an important role. In this chapter, I share the approach I use to help leaders increase self-awareness, change their behavior, and hold themselves accountable.

CHANGE BEGINS WITH SELF-AWARENESS AND REFLECTION

Being aware of how a leader is, perhaps unintentionally, building or reinforcing the current culture is essential for culture change to be successful. It is this self-awareness that makes it possible to identify the changes certain leaders need to make in their own behaviors, the direction they provide to others, and their decisions. However, identifying the behaviors the leaders need to stop and start demonstrating is just the beginning. The leaders must then actually make the necessary adjustments, which means being aware of their actions so they can hold themselves accountable.

Achieving this level of self-awareness requires that the leader take the time to engage in reflection not just at the beginning but throughout the culture change process. One technique that can be helpful is guided reflection.[22] Guided reflection is the process of using questions to critically examine our actions, assumptions, and motives. It helps us to be honest with ourselves, and it can also provide insights regarding our biases and feelings and how these affect our actions and decisions.

For guided reflection to be effective, it is important to establish context and ask the right questions. When using the CASPE culture change process, the context is how the current culture is causing a problem for the business. Specifically, what it is about the current culture that is interfering with strategy execution or causing another problem? With this made clear, the leader will be ready to answer questions designed to help them identify if and how their actions are contributing to the problem.

Context

To illustrate the logic and how the conversation with a leader might unfold, we continue with the E&M case study, specifically as it concerns Caroline, the business unit leader I was asked to coach. To recap, E&M's siloed culture, which had contributed to the company's past success, had become a problem and needed to change if the company was to win competitive bids requiring a solution that integrated the products and services from its three business units. However, for this to happen, Caroline and the other business unit leaders needed to work together to break down the silos and increase collaboration between their teams. While Caroline was saying the right things, her actions were not consistent with her words. This is the reason the CHRO called me. She and Michel, the CEO, believed that Caroline was the problem.

Eventually, they came to realize the problem was much bigger than Caroline. The siloed culture of the company was evident in every aspect of its operations, from its strategy to the way it was structured and the design of processes, systems, policies, procedures, and so on. That said, Caroline, as a senior executive, controlled or influenced most if not all of these elements. Her decisions, as well as her behavior, shaped the culture within her business unit and, to an extent, the rest of the organization. While the CHRO and CEO were reasonably confident that Caroline's participation in the CASPE process would help, they were concerned she lacked self-awareness, which would cause her to unintentionally undermine the change effort. As a result, they decided to provide Caroline with coaching in parallel with the CASPE process. The advantage of this tandem approach is that the discussions that happen during the CASPE process naturally encourage leaders to reflect on their behavior and actions. By providing coaching, you can build on this to deepen insights and increase self-awareness, eventually leading to changes in behavior and other actions required to intentionally build the culture the organization needs.

Ideally, coaching is provided to every leader who is actively involved in the CASPE process. In E&M's case, this would include, at a minimum, the three business unit leaders, as they were involved in all phases. When the leaders are executives, I strongly recommend engaging an external coach for the reasons cited earlier. If they hold lower-level positions, coaching can be effectively delivered by experienced internal HR/OD coaches using the same approach and questions. However, it is important that the coaches, be they internal or external, have a deep understanding of culture and the CASPE process as well as the outcomes from the phase one and two workshops. This is necessary for them to ask the right probing questions and help the leader make the connection between their actions, others' behavior, and the culture of their team and organization.

Guided Reflection Questions

Five questions are used to guide the reflective process:

1. Why have you encouraged the way things are done currently?
2. What are you doing to encourage the current way of working?
3. What changes do you need to make to encourage different behaviors and ways of working?
4. What would stop you from making these changes?
5. How are you going to hold yourself accountable?

The phrasing of the questions is intentionally generic; however, when asking them, the coach should make specific reference to relevant content identified in the CASPE workshops. For example, the first question asks the leader, "Why have you encouraged the way things are done currently?" In Caroline's case, I would rephrase this to read, "Why have you encouraged the people in your business unit to work independently of the other business units?" Alternatively, I could take a more diplomatic approach and say something like, "I am sure there are very good reasons why your business unit doesn't work closely with the other units. It would be very helpful if you could explain this to me." Both options are good, but my recommendation is to always take a diplomatic approach, as it is less likely to trigger a defensive response.

If the leader struggles to answer the questions, suggest that they ask people they work and interact with on a regular basis for their input. In fact, sharing their answers with people they know and trust is a good way to validate their observations, potentially reveal blind spots (we all have them), and provide other insights.

Question #1—Why have you encouraged the way things are done currently?

Understanding what drives behavior is essential if behaviors are to change. Remember, beliefs drive behavior, and a leader's behavior and actions influence others' behaviors and build culture. If the leader's beliefs remain unchanged, chances are that person won't sustain the needed changes to behavior, and the culture change effort will fail.

In phase one, leaders discuss how the company's culture is causing or contributing to the business problem. This is followed in phase two with identifying the current way of working, which includes behaviors. Both discussions can provide insights into leaders' behaviors and actions, as well as the reasons for them. This is why I recommend asking this question after phase two is completed. For the conversation to be productive, it is important that the leaders have the right mindset.

They need to accept that the way they did things in the past was effective and right for that time but now something has happened, a triggering event, that means things need to be done differently.

Caroline, contrary to what the CEO and CHRO had anticipated, was very open and receptive to coaching and engaged fully in our conversation. She immediately said that her priority, and that of the other business unit leaders, was to achieve her business's goals and targets. This is what determined her and her team's performance and most of their compensation, including bonuses. In addition, the company allocated resources, including funds for capital projects, based on business unit results, which encouraged competition, not collaboration. Yes, the business units competed, and this led, at times, to some not-so-great behavior, but they achieved what the company needed, which was results.

Furthermore, she explained that the business units were very different. They had different processes, structures, policies, and so on that had proven to be effective. There wasn't integration because it wasn't needed. She trusted her colleagues to run their business units, and they trusted her to do the same. So long as they all delivered what they needed to deliver, everyone wins. This isn't to say that they didn't work together, because they did. As members of E&M's executive team, they were responsible for developing and implementing strategy. They also met regularly to discuss other issues affecting the company, but this did not include matters specific to their business units. That said, she acknowledged they needed to do some things differently. Each of their businesses was losing revenue because they weren't providing customers with an integrated solution. She agreed with the other leaders that the business units needed to work together if they were to solve the problem. In reaching this decision, Caroline made an important shift in her perspective and, in doing so, took the first step toward changing the culture.

Question #2—What are you doing to encourage the current way of working?

With this question, we want the leader to identify the specific things they are doing to encourage current behaviors and reinforce that this is the right and expected way to do things. In my experience, most leaders have no difficulty providing several, if not numerous, examples. Your job is to help them go deeper and talk about why they are doing these things.

The exact question I asked Caroline was, "I would like you to think about what it is you are doing that encourages people to work independently and discourages them from assisting or collaborating with other business units. For example, we heard that employees in all three business units were not responsive to requests for information or assistance from the other units. How might you be encouraging this?"

Caroline began by saying every person who reported to her had goals and targets that were aligned with those of the business unit. She made it clear that this, and only this, would be the basis for their performance rating and bonus. She went on to say she had also put policies in place to restrict access to her business's information databases, including its customer relationship management (CRM) system and pricing database. Members of the other business units could not access these systems, and she had instructed that this information was not to be provided to anyone outside of her business unit without her approval. When I asked why, she explained that the other business units competed for the business of some of their customers. She did not want to give them information that would help them at the expense of her business unit. When asked if she thought this was the best way of doing things, she replied to the effect of, "Maybe not, but this is the way things have been done for a long time. Until recently, there hadn't been any reason to change. And, by the way, the other business units do the same thing."

When Caroline was finished speaking, I asked her to think about the complaints she had heard from other groups, or her own team, about the current way of doing things. This is also a good question to ask if a leader struggles with the original wording. If the leader hesitates, draw on examples identified during CASPE discussions. For example, I had heard several executives complain that Caroline's team wasn't responsive to their requests for information and assistance. When I asked her how she might be contributing to this, she said she suspected her team was giving priority to work within the business unit, which meant requests from other business units were dealt with when and if people had the time.

If the leader is unsure or can't answer the question, I suggest that they canvas the people on their team. Keep in mind that, if the behaviors other leaders are complaining about happen often and are exhibited by multiple people, there is always a reason, which is usually that they believe it is acceptable. However, it is important to note that people, especially at lower levels, may be reluctant to provide a leader, especially an executive, with direct feedback. To get around this, I suggest either myself or an HR/OD professional interview people on the leader's team. This is usually perceived as less threatening, which can encourage people to be more forthcoming and candid.

Question #3—What changes do you need to make to encourage different behaviors and ways of working?

While the first two questions focus on their current state, this question is about the future and the changes the leader needs to make to close the culture gap and solve the problem. Their answer should include changes to their own behavior and practices, not just to policies or processes, which is usually their first inclination. After all, these are much easier to change. To some extent, this occurs naturally as a product of adjusting beliefs to accommodate an alternative or expanded worldview. When this happens, leaders change the way they talk about things and make decisions that are aligned with their new perspective. However, being intentional in their choices and actions makes their efforts more effective.

How does intentionality make a leader more effective? For one, most of us have a limited capacity for change, which means we need to focus our energy and attention on those changes that will have the greatest impact. Second, the changes involve behavior and, as we know, this is not easy. When it comes to behavior, it is better to identify a select few (I recommend one at a time but definitely no more than three) and focus on these for sixty-six days or until they become a habit.[23] The more specific the behaviors are, the better.

To help with this, I ask the leader to focus on the specific pain point that was identified in phase one of the CASPE process. At E&M, this was the failure to prepare an integrated response to customers' RFPs. This can narrow the list of behaviors and practices the leader identifies to a critical few. In Caroline's case, I started by asking her to identify a few behaviors and practices she was going to start and stop doing to show she was serious about improving collaboration between the business units. As expected, her initial answers were fairly general. For example, she told me that when there was an issue with another business unit or a corporate function, she tended to jump to her team's defense. Similarly, she knew she advocated strongly for things that were in her business unit's interests and didn't support decisions that negatively impacted her team's ability to achieve its financial targets. She committed to do a better job of listening and asking questions before arriving at a conclusion or making a decision.

I then got very specific and asked her what she could start or stop doing to show she was serious about collaborating with the other business units to prepare an integrated response to customers' RFPs. Her first response was to assign people on her team to work with the other business units; however, she then said she was already doing this. I then asked if there was anything else she could do differently to improve the level of collaboration that was happening. She admitted that while she had assigned someone to work with another business unit on a customer proposal, she gave clear instructions that they were to make sure the terms of the proposal were advantageous to her business unit. While it was important that her business unit's goals and targets were met, she indicated she could do a better job of providing direction to her team. Once she had a comprehensive list of the things she could stop or start doing, I asked her to prioritize them and identify no more than three she was going to act on starting immediately.

Question #4—What would stop you from making these changes?

The reality is that with every change effort, things are going to happen that challenge even the best of intentions. The trick is for the leader to recognize when this occurs and be prepared to act appropriately. One way to accomplish this is to help the leader draw on past experience to identify the challenges they might face. This does not need to be an exhaustive exercise. Focus on one to three things they suspect are likely to happen. If there are more, that's also fine. Once the list is created, ask the leader what they are going to do when this happens and suggest that they write it down. This will act as a cue to help them respond appropriately if it happens.

In Caroline's case, her business unit was under intense pressure to achieve its financial targets. The shift toward integrated solutions was having the greatest impact on her business. Revenues were down, and her team was struggling to find a way to recoup them. While she recognized that to win a competitive bid for an integrated solution, her business unit might need to lower its prices, she was concerned this would make the problem worse. If this happened, and her team failed to achieve their financial targets, they would be in a weaker position when it came time to compete for resources, including investments in the capital projects required to grow the business. Furthermore, the people on her team wouldn't get their year-end bonuses, which would have a massive negative impact on morale. While there wasn't an obvious solution, she decided that if this happened, she would increase her efforts to have the goals changed and ask for assistance from HR in addressing the bonus issue.

Related to this, she also identified that competing opportunities and demands could tempt her to pull people away from working on the joint submission to focus on business unit-specific initiatives. Resource allocation was always a challenge, especially when there was so much pressure to improve performance. If this happened, she committed to meeting with the other business unit leaders to identify options. If, after discussion, it was determined her business unit's resources were needed on the joint team, she would honor the decision.

If you are coaching the managers or executives, it is important to help them be proactive and identify these types of situations and variables and even more important to work with them to identify a concrete set of actions to take if they arise. By articulating and, preferably, documenting the actions they commit to take, you create a tool that can be used to encourage higher levels of accountability.

Question #5—How are you going to hold yourself accountable?

This leads us to the final question, which is about accountability. Most of us unconsciously demonstrate a wide range of behaviors as we go about our day. We get busy, things happen, and, without realizing it, we fall back into old ways of doing things. If we are under pressure or involved in a crisis, it is even more likely we will break our commitments and revert to old behaviors. While no one expects a leader to be perfect, they are held to a higher standard. Remember, people create meaning out of everything a leader says and does. If the leader behaves in a manner that is inconsistent with what they are telling others is important, they are going to raise doubts that can impact others' behavior and choices. This is why it is important to quickly recognize when this happens and take action to get back on track.

There are a few things you can suggest to a leader that might help. The first is to write down the behaviors and other changes they have committed to make and place this somewhere they see them at the start of the workday. This might be on the home screen of their computer or mobile device, a framed card on their desk, or a sticky note attached to their monitor. To emphasize how important this is, I make a point of asking them to email their commitments to me, and I have them printed on postcards that I give to them. It doesn't matter how they do it, they just need to do it. The important thing is that they have a constant reminder of their commitments, so they are primed to be aware of their behavior and the implications of their actions.

The second thing the leader can do is to share their commitments with a few people they know and trust and who work with them enough to see them in action on a regular basis. This is called an accountability circle. The leader then asks the people in their accountability circle to let them know when they do something that is consistent or inconsistent with these commitments. If they agree, the leader should plan to follow up with them occasionally to ask for feedback. Again, this doesn't need to be a big deal. Simply asking questions as part of normal interactions, such as after a meeting or at the end of a call, is all that is necessary. Initially, people may be reticent to provide feedback that isn't positive, but with time, and if the leader isn't defensive, they should open up and offer helpful suggestions. At a minimum, sharing intentions and following up is a great way for leaders to hold themselves accountable for doing what they say they are going to do.

Another thing I encourage leaders to do is to use a journal to capture their thoughts and insights. This is not restricted to the CASPE process. Keep in mind that the objective is to gain insights into the leaders' behavior, the reasons for the decisions they are making, and how these influence others' behavior and actions. This doesn't need to be an onerous exercise. Just a few notes and observations can help to imprint insights, which can increase self-awareness and help with learning new behaviors. You can also suggest they do this at the same time of day every day, which, for most people, is at the end of the workday. Suggest the leaders start by reviewing their commitments and then ask themselves, "What did I do well, what can I do better, and what am I going to do differently tomorrow?" Unfortunately, even when positioned this way, I have found that most leaders dislike journaling or find it difficult to make the time to do it. If this happens, I ask them to try it for one week to see if it helps.

A FINAL THOUGHT

On occasion, someone will ask if a leader can answer these questions without the assistance of a coach. The short answer is yes . . . if the leader is reflective, self-critical, observant, and self-aware. They must also be motivated to change and can be counted on to put in the time and effort required. If you are confident the leader meets these criteria, then I would ask them to read chapter two, the power of intentional leadership, as well as this chapter, and offer to meet with them to discuss their answers and experience when they are ready.

That said, it is more common for the answer to be no. Reflecting on behavior and the reasons for it is not easy or natural for most of us, which is why it can be helpful to engage an external or internal coach. A coach can ask the tough questions that encourage the leaders to be honest with themselves, challenge their thinking, and push them to recognize what they need to do differently and why. The coach can also help the leaders to follow through on their commitments and hold themselves accountable. This will not only increase the probability that the leaders will change their behavior and the culture, but it can also help them to further develop their leadership skills. Ultimately, whether the leaders make the changes that are needed is up to them. However, it is important they know that, if they don't change, it is likely efforts to change the culture will fail.

CHAPTER NINE

FACILITATION AND OTHER TIPS

BEFORE WE GO ANY further, I want to share some tips for running the CASPE workshops. These are things I have learned and obstacles I have encountered and overcome over the years. This may be a refresher for some, especially those of you who are skilled facilitators with experience working with groups of senior leaders.

GENERAL ADVICE AND TIPS

Tip #1 — Make it clear the leader, not HR/OD, is leading the culture change.

As you know, culture change does not happen unless leaders own it and are actively involved in making it happen. Yet, most people, regardless of their level, assume that if an initiative has anything to do with culture, then HR/OD is in charge. If this assumption remains throughout the attempted change, it is the kiss of death. Even the perception that HR/OD is leading the change can undermine the effectiveness of the change effort. I have found that the best way to deal with this is to assume this is what people are thinking and address it directly. Even before the first workshop, it is important for the leaders to emphasize that they are leading the initiative and that the role of HR/OD is to provide support. This support might include facilitating the working sessions, since it is difficult to lead, facilitate, and participate in discussions concurrently.

Tip #2—Anticipate questions and objections.

As the CASPE process is about changing culture, people may ask you things like "What do you mean by culture?" or "How do we know culture is the problem?" You need to be prepared to answer these types of questions. My advice is to keep your answers concise and straightforward, such as "Culture is the way we do things here." Use an example they can relate to, preferably something positive, and stay away from saying anything about the culture problem, as they need to be the ones to identify this. For instance, "We have a 'family' culture, and we are caring and supportive, which is one of the reasons people enjoy working here. While this is something we value and want to protect, it does cause us a few problems, such as we tend to avoid conflict and debate, which are needed to generate more and better ideas."

You may also hear objections such as "Why are we here? Isn't this HR's job?" This is a question the leader should answer by reminding them that they are here to solve a business problem they and other leaders believe is caused by a gap in the culture. Solving business problems is a business leader's job, not HR's. Business leaders are accountable for the company's P&L, not HR. They know the business at a detailed level and why things are done the way they are, not HR. For example, the leader may say "This is our problem, and we need to solve it. If this means we must change the culture, then we are the ones to do it. Of course, we will need support and guidance, which is where HR is going to help."

Whatever the questions are, my advice is to be prepared. Generate a list of the objections you might hear, assign them to the leader or facilitator, and prepare your answers in advance. This will help to prevent the discussion from being sidetracked or derailed.

Tip #3 — In-person is better than virtual.

It is possible to conduct the working sessions virtually; however, I find it more effective for people to meet face-to-face. This is because discussions often deal with issues that have gone unresolved for a long time. By the time you get to the point of considering culture change as a possible solution, you've likely exhausted every other option. However, when problems and issues linger, interpersonal conflicts, blaming, and other challenges often emerge, which increases people's sensitivity to criticism. Although the discussions are focused on *what* rather than *who*, this can result in defensive behaviors, causing individuals to withdraw and not engage.

Another obvious benefit of having people meet face-to-face is it strengthens connections and relationships. When embarking on culture change, this can be important, as it allows a community or network to emerge that people can tap into if they have questions or encounter obstacles. As the community grows, it can become a source of support as well as information and ideas, which are especially valuable when the change efforts expand in scope and scale.

That said, if face-to-face sessions are not possible, holding them virtually using apps such as Microsoft Teams or Zoom is a viable option. If this happens, be aware that you will need to build in more time for discussions. Additionally, the length of the working sessions should not exceed three hours, which can cause the number of sessions to increase. Regardless, it is important that the working sessions in each phase are conducted close together to minimize knowledge and information loss and maintain momentum.

Tip #4 — To encourage candor, keep the discussion focused on facts.

The secret to achieving the level of candor needed for the CASPE process to be effective is to keep the discussions objective and focused on the facts. However, because people are talking about behavior, this can sometimes trigger defensiveness and resentment, especially if there are festering issues. There are a few things you can do to try to prevent this from happening.

The first is to remind everyone the current culture and way of doing things exist for a reason, which is that they have helped the company to succeed. However, things have changed, such as the expectations of national and global customers (as was the case for E&M), which means the team must do things differently if they are to continue to thrive and grow. Second, remind them that it is important to assume positive intent. If people behave or do things a certain way, it is because they believe it is the right way to do things and is in the best interests of the organization. Suggest that, instead of making assumptions, they try listening so they understand the person's perspective and the reasons for their behavior. Third, and related to positive intent, avoid talking about who is causing the problem, which usually comes across as blaming. This happens frequently when giving examples to illustrate behaviors. Instead, talk about what is causing the problem. While it can be tempting to use names, as this can provide context, try to avoid it. It is better to refer to a department, project, or task, as this depersonalizes the event, making it more likely people will be willing to discuss it.

CASPE PRO TIPS: PHASE ONE

Tip #5 — Test for alignment and commitment before moving forward.

One of the objectives of phase one is to confirm leaders are aligned in their understanding of the business problem and in agreement that the culture needs to change to solve it. Without this alignment, there is no sense in continuing with the CASPE process or the change effort. The commitment needed for it to be successful simply isn't there. I also recommend checking that the alignment and commitment continue throughout the process so that, if this changes, you can bring it to the leaders' attention and address it.

There are different ways to check for alignment, but the approach I find works best is to ask people to write their answers to a question on index cards and post them on a wall. The group then gathers around the posted cards and discusses the content. This allows us to check for consistency and identify any answers that are out of alignment or unclear. If everyone has written the same thing, which occasionally happens, I ask for someone to read their answer and explain it to the group. As they read it, I write the answer on a flip chart and then ask if everyone agrees or if further clarification is needed. While this may seem repetitive, it is another check and balance. Also, by writing the answer in big letters and posting it on the wall, it can be referred to throughout the meeting.

This not only focuses the discussion but is also a great way to surface assumptions. While you may think everyone is on the same page and shares the same perspective, this is often not the case. Even if people are using the same words, the meaning and interpretation can be different. One way to test for this is to ask each person to answer the question one at a time. Avoid offering your perspective and hold questions and discussion until everyone has spoken. This will tell you where things stand before you go any further. Obviously, the challenge is that this takes time. If possible, I recommend to at least check for alignment regarding their perspective on the culture problem.

In my experience, most leaders are aligned on the business problem. There were likely already multiple meetings and endless discussions before they got to the point where they were even willing to consider the cause might be a gap in the culture. The challenge is in reaching an agreement that the culture is the problem and what exactly it is about the culture that is causing the problem. If leaders are not aligned, it can be helpful to go back to the business problem and then ask the question in a different way, such as "How is our culture contributing to or causing this problem?" Remember, the culture needs to change for a reason. It is interfering with strategy execution or otherwise preventing the organization from achieving its goals. If people say their culture needs to change, ask them why. Why does your culture need to change? What problem is it causing now? The answer had better be compelling; if it's not, don't go any further. Without a compelling reason to change the culture, other priorities and demands will take precedence. It will be a nice-to-do task and will fail.

Tip #6—Identify the right pain point.

The third question in phase one asks leaders to identify where the culture is causing the most pain. At E&M, this was the lack of an integrated response to customer RFPs that asked for solutions requiring products and services from its three business units. As a result, they had failed to win a competitive bid in the previous twelve months and were losing revenue and market share. The pain point was obvious, but this is not always the case. It is, however, the type of situation you should be looking for.

First, it is compelling and, if solved, will have a significant positive impact on the business. Beyond the obvious benefits, this situation has the potential to provide proof that CASPE works and that there is value in scaling it to drive change in other parts of the business. Second, it challenges people to think differently about the best way to do things (beliefs) and requires new and different behaviors or ways of working. In other words, it requires a culture change to solve the problem. Third, it is sufficiently contained, manageable and not overly complex, which means it can be implemented within three to four months. The last thing you want is to select a situation that is so complex and large in scope that it takes too long to implement. Not only does this increase the risk that you will encounter problems that are difficult to overcome but people will likely lose interest. Finally, it needs to be work that is going to happen regardless of whether it is part of the CASPE process. This ensures that it is important, relevant, and sustainable. Creating a special project or initiative is rarely effective.

Tip #7—Use the culture-strategy alignment model to conclude phase one.

An effective way to bring phase one to a conclusion is to use the culture-strategy alignment model to summarize the discussion and outcomes (see chapter five). This will provide a clear visual representation of how the current culture is interfering with strategy execution and causing a problem for the business that can be referred to throughout the change effort.

Start by explaining the model, using an example the team can relate to. This should not be the current situation the team is discussing but something that is contextually relevant and gets the point across. One such example is provided in chapter five, with the case of AVSC, the advanced video solutions company. You could ask people to read the chapter in preparation for the meeting. If you decide to go with this option, just be aware that people may not do so, and you will need to explain it. The next step is to facilitate a discussion with the team to complete the model or, alternatively, show one that you completed during the session (see diagram 7 in chapter seven). With the model complete, check that everyone agrees it is an accurate summary of the discussion and confirm the specific business problem that will be the focus going forward. Make it clear that there is no going back. If anyone has any concerns, this is the time to say so.

CASPE PRO TIPS: PHASE TWO

Tip #8—Identify the behaviors needed to solve the problem.

In phase two, leaders are asked to identify what they will see people doing when the problem is solved. Think of this as a visioning and brainstorming exercise. If all is right with the world and the problem is solved—for example, the company is winning competitive bids for integrated solutions—how are people behaving and what are they doing? How are they working together? What other behaviors are we seeing? At E&M, the CEO who was leading the discussion decided to be direct and put what he believed was the obvious solution on the table. Specifically, he told the leaders, "When the problem is solved, I would see salespeople from all three business units working on the response to the RFP together," to which, as a facilitator, I turned to the group and asked, "How will we see people behaving and what will they be doing when they are working together effectively?"

If you are facilitating, don't restrict the idea-generation process and avoid critiquing until all the ideas are on the table. If people struggle to come up with ideas, an easy way to get the discussion started is to refer to the behaviors that leaders said need to change and ask, "If this is the way we do things now, what do people need to continue doing and what new or different behaviors will we see?" In most cases, once people understand what you're looking for and get engaged in the discussion, you can let the conversation go in whatever direction the group takes it, so long as it stays focused on the problem scenario. In the end, they should have a solid list of behaviors.

Tip #9 — When using CASPE for the first time, select one scenario as the pilot.

By narrowing the focus to one specific situation—in E&M's case, one RFP response—fewer people need to be involved, which is less logistically challenging and more realistic. The managers and employees participating in the pilot will need to commit to a more rigorous approach to project management and a higher degree of visibility than normal. They may also have to learn new ways of working and behaving. The pilot also requires the active involvement of senior leaders; HR/OD professionals; and possibly a CASPE expert, who will observe the team, participate in team discussions, remove barriers, and provide formal and informal updates to senior leaders who are not directly involved in the pilot. It is unrealistic to expect that these people will be able to dedicate the time this requires to more than one pilot.

Importantly, it is also easier for people to identify the specific details that need to be addressed for the solution to be successful when they focus on one distinct and very real situation. Also, if you are implementing the CASPE process for the first time, you and the other people involved are learning how to use it and don't need it to be more complicated than necessary.

Finally, most leaders are skeptical that culture change is even possible in a reasonable time frame, never mind that it will resolve an important business problem. This is why it is important to provide evidence that offers proof the process works.

Tip #10—When there are multiple possible pilot scenarios, use decision criteria to select the best option.

There are many ways to approach selecting the scenario to use as the pilot, but I have found that the following tends to work consistently well. The first step is to ask the workshop participants to generate a list of the active occurrences of the pain point. For example, at E&M, there were three active customer RFPs that required an integrated solution. From this list, the participants are asked to identify those that are most urgent and important but that would also provide a test of the full process and potential proof of concept. While there isn't an exact target number, most groups identify between three and five.

The next step is to identify the criteria to use to select the pilot. I start with the criteria in tip #6, then ask the team if there is anything else that needs to be added. If you want, you can then rate the criteria from one to ten, which allows those that are most important to have greater influence on the outcome. I decide whether to do this based on the discussion that occurs. For example, if the team says that one criterion is less important than another and shouldn't have the same impact on the outcome, then I include criteria weighting.

With the criteria identified, I ask the team to rate the short list of potential pilots using a scale from one to ten, with one being the least important and ten being the most important. The results are combined and the overall scores calculated. As an aside, I use one of the many software applications available for this, as it makes the exercise quick and easy. Once the results are tabulated, I ask the people who selected an option other than the one that received the highest score to explain why they voted the way they did. In some cases, as at E&M, one situation receives significantly higher scores than the other options. However, even in this case, it is worth taking a few minutes to discuss the results and give people the opportunity to explain their answers. There have been instances where a lower-scored option ended up being selected because a compelling argument convinced the rest of the team to change the decision. Finally, with a decision made, you are ready to conclude this step with a call to action.

CASPE PRO TIP: PHASE THREE

Tip #11 — Identify what could stop people from changing their behavior.

One of the questions in phase three asks managers to identify what would prevent behavior from changing. The objective is to identify as many obstacles as possible, large and small, and then develop a plan to address them. If the obstacles are "game stoppers," they need to be actioned before anything else can happen. I have found that the most common ones are misaligned goals and rewards, lack of resources and support, competing demands, and excessive workloads. Most of the time, groups tend to have no difficulty answering the question; however, this is not always the case. If this happens, it can help to reword the question, such as, "What would stop this (the solution or change) from happening?" For example, at E&M, the managers said that senior leaders could pull team members off the integrated RFP response team (the solution) to do business unit-specific work.

Once the list of obstacles is complete, it is important to allow enough time for participants to discuss and clarify what and why these are relevant before moving into solutions. While this is happening, the senior leaders in the room need to ask questions and listen to understand the team's concerns and avoid doing or saying anything that could be perceived as minimizing, avoiding the issue, or defensiveness. When the team has finished, it is appropriate to ask the leaders if there are any items that can be decided now and what those are and to share their answers and rationale with the team. As a side note, I recommend calling a break before this discussion so the leaders have time to huddle before being called upon to make a decision. If the leaders agree, I also like to have the huddle happen in the room with the team present, as this encourages transparency and can build trust. Of course, this depends on the leaders' comfort level and the nature of the team's concerns. For example, volatile issues may be raised that are best not discussed in front of the team to avoid misperceptions or a negative backlash. These can always be parked with the promise that a decision will be made at a later date; however, if the concern is a hot issue, then doing this and addressing others can be perceived negatively. In this situation, I recommend that the leaders huddle privately so they can decide how best to address the team's concerns. Finally, before ending the discussion, review the list of obstacles and actions to be taken and make sure it is clear who is responsible for each item and when a decision is expected, if it hasn't been made at the workshop.

Tip #12—To measure culture, identify an outcome that can only be achieved by changing behavior.

I often get asked how a company can measure culture change. The answer is when people are consistently demonstrating the behaviors that you want to see. This indicates that they believe this is the right and expected way to do things. As noted earlier, meaningful and sustainable change in behavior takes, on average, sixty-six days to achieve. You could assess this shift using behavioral assessment methods, such as observation, but that is highly subjective and can fail to identify subtle indicators that the new behaviors are not established. Alternatively, you can use a culture survey to conduct a pre- and post-measure; however, these are broad and lack the sensitivity to assess detailed and subtle changes in behavior. The better option is to identify an outcome that can only be achieved by changing behavior, such as an improvement in customer experience, which was the measure used at E&M.

WATCH OUT FOR LAND MINES!

Despite our best efforts, almost every change effort, including the CASPE process, has its share of land mines, the challenges that lurk below the surface that, if we don't defuse them properly, will blow up in our face. In the next chapter, I share some of the land mines I have encountered and what I have done to make sure they don't happen in the future.

CHAPTER TEN
LAND MINES AND HOW TO AVOID THEM

As with any major change initiative, stuff is bound to happen. You can't avoid all of it, but if you know what to watch for, you can take steps to mitigate the damage. That is what this chapter is about—knowing where the land mines are and putting plans in place so, if you trigger one, you are ready to act.

LAND MINE #1: COMPETING DEMANDS AND DISTRACTIONS

The number one reason culture change efforts fail is that the leaders accountable for the change don't follow through. There are so many demands competing for their time and attention that, without fully realizing it, they no longer observe and interact with people or attend weekly check-ins and planning and review meetings. Maybe they delegate this to a lower-level manager, or perhaps they do nothing at all. The same applies to changing their own behavior. Like everyone else, this takes energy and attention consistently applied for at least sixty-six days or until the new behavior becomes a habit.

The problem with this goes back to the point I have made time and again, which is that for meaningful and sustained culture change to happen, leaders must personally own and actively participate in all aspects of the change effort. No matter what they say, unless they lead the way, others will continue to do things and behave the way they always have. This is something that you as an HR/OD professional can help with. While you can't do things for them, you can observe leaders' behavior and engage with them to ensure they are aware of their actions and make the necessary adjustments.

Knowing this is a reality most leaders face, identifying what and how they are going to prevent themselves from reverting to old behaviors can help. One way is to use the practices suggested in the previous chapter, but if this isn't appealing or they don't think these will work for them, encourage them to try something else. For example, they could ask you, or perhaps their team, for help in holding them accountable. They could also consider asking a trusted colleague they work with on a regular basis to do this. The important thing is to do something so that if a lapse happens, the leader is aware of it as early as possible and takes the steps required to address it.

LAND MINE #2: UNEXPECTED TROUBLE

Sometimes, unexpected things happen that need to be addressed because of their potential to derail the change effort. These are the distractions or competing demands that must be dealt with. This can be an existing issue or something entirely new that affects the people or work involved in the CASPE process. We ran into this at E&M when a long-simmering employee relations issue threatened to derail the pilot.

Members of E&M's sales teams were very unhappy with the company's practice of ranking individuals based on the revenue they generated and using this to determine performance ratings and compensation. However, what brought matters to a head was the decision to terminate the bottom 10 percent of performers in each team based on revenue. This was announced early on in phase four and brought all activity concerning the pilot to a halt. The salespeople refused to engage until the issue was resolved to their satisfaction. Eventually, a decision was made to temporarily rescind the new policy with the promise that the sales teams would be consulted before further action was taken. While this didn't completely satisfy people, it was sufficient to convince them to move forward.

In this case, there was no question that the issue had to be dealt with immediately. There are, however, others that are less obvious but just as important to act on because of the risk they create for the change effort. The good news is these are usually easy to detect, as many will be voiced, perhaps subtly, in the discussion of challenges in implementing the changes that are needed. You can also uncover them by walking around and observing and interacting with the team. If the issue is causing angst or creating a significant problem, you'll hear people talking about it or behaving in a way you didn't expect. When this happens, the best approach is usually to gather the people affected or involved together, ask questions, and listen to understand their perspectives and suggestions. The last thing you want is for issues to lead to resentment and discontent that negatively affect the dynamics within the team and their performance.

LAND MINE #3: TAKING SHORTCUTS AND JUMPING TO CONCLUSIONS

Leaders are under pressure to get results and, being skilled problem solvers, sometimes tend to fast-forward through a discussion or process, especially when they think they know the answer. They want to get to solutions and actions as quickly as possible. If you are facilitating, it is important to be aware and watch for this, as they may try to pressure or convince you to speed things up by perhaps skipping a question or cutting conversations short.

The questions and activities that are part of the CASPE process are necessary to make the right decisions and ultimately solve the business problem. Skipping questions or cutting a conversation short will negatively affect the outcome and potentially the entire change effort. To address this, I recommend that, at the beginning and throughout the process, you remind people that success requires following the process in its entirety. If people push back, explain that the reason they are here is because the company has a major problem that needs to be solved and they decided this was how they were going to do it. If they still insist on reducing time, you can suggest reducing the time for each workshop; however, make it clear that doing so will likely require additional sessions to achieve the desired outcome. Whatever you do, do not agree to removing questions. These have been carefully selected because they are necessary to get the desired results.

LAND MINE #4: MAKING ASSUMPTIONS

Assumptions are a form of taking a shortcut that happen because someone believes they know what others are thinking or that other people interpret things the same way they do. While this is normal behavior, failure to clarify assumptions can lead to miscommunication, misunderstanding, and disagreement. Unfortunately, detecting assumptions can be tricky, and asking for clarification can be even trickier, as people, especially senior leaders, can become impatient.

My advice is to steel yourself and stay the course. In particular, listen for words or phrases that are value-laden, vague, or otherwise open to interpretation, as these can often mean

different things to different people. For example, when someone says the teams need to collaborate more or better, what
do they mean? For one person, this might mean that a specific team needs to consult with another team before making
decisions, while someone else might interpret this as meaning
teams need to engage in joint problem-solving and make decisions together.

LAND MINE #5: MESSY INTERPERSONAL DYNAMICS AND TRUST ISSUES

Sometimes, culture problems are accompanied by interpersonal conflicts, funky team dynamics, political agendas, inappropriate behavior, trust issues, and other messy stuff. If this is
the case in your company, chances are pretty good that these
conflicts are going to surface during the CASPE process, which
means that, if you are facilitating, you need to be prepared to
deal with it. Of course, you could try to ignore it, but that rarely works, if ever, as ignoring problematic behavior usually only
makes the situation worse. When this happens, it can negatively affect the quality of discussion that takes place during the
CASPE process. This can undermine the effectiveness of the
process and negatively impact the outcome.

It can help to establish norms for behavior in the phase one
workshop; review these at the start of each phase, working session, and meeting; and end meetings or working sessions with
a review of how well the norms were followed. An alternative
is to address the behavior when it happens by stopping the discussion; calling for a break; and, in a direct manner, making
it clear the behavior is unacceptable. A third option is to have
an external consultant who is certified in the CASPE process
facilitate the working sessions and meetings. Of course, not

all facilitators are created equal. If you know or suspect that messy interpersonal dynamics or inappropriate behavior could interfere, make sure the facilitator has the skills to deal with this. Regardless of what you decide, be alert to the warning signs and have a plan in place to deal with them. Avoidance and inaction will only lead to failure.

LAND MINE #6: ORGANIZATIONAL POLITICS

Politics are a fact of life in virtually every organization. While they can serve a positive purpose, such as building connections and strengthening relationships, they can also be disruptive. This happens when individuals do things that are motivated by personal gain, sometimes at the expense of others. For example, someone might lobby to be part of the CASPE process because it provides exposure to senior leaders they wouldn't otherwise have.

At E&M, politics raised its head on several occasions, mostly when decisions were made that involved power and status. For example, there was a lengthy and heated discussion as to who should lead the pilot team. In this instance, each business unit leader lobbied hard for someone on their team with the belief this would give more power to their business unit than the others. As with navigating messy interpersonal and team dynamics, organizational politics can be difficult to manage. The most effective strategy is to proactively communicate how decisions are going to be made and, if appropriate, the criteria that should be applied at the beginning of the process. This way, people can make their arguments and advocate for their ideas with the understanding that once a decision is made, they are expected to support it. At E&M, the situation was resolved by identifying decision criteria, which the CEO, CHRO, and business unit leaders used to evaluate the candidates. Although the business unit leaders each rated their person higher, the cumulative result led to the right candidate being selected.

LAND MINE #7: PASSIVE-AGGRESSIVE AND DEFENSIVE BEHAVIOR

Some questions, especially in phases one and two, can involve discussions that trigger defensiveness and passive-aggressive behavior. Usually, this is a product of long-held disagreements and resentment that have been allowed to fester. However, it can also be caused because the answer to a posed question, although obvious to some, conflicts with a leader's beliefs as to the best or right way of doing things. A good indicator that this is happening is if someone is not participating in the discussion and contributing ideas or is being overly critical.

Predictably, this happened at E&M. It was predictable because the initiative began with the CHRO telling me that they had a problem with one of the business unit leaders, Caroline, who refused to collaborate with the others. Caroline was a very smart person and wasn't overtly obstructive or disruptive, especially with her boss, the CEO, leading the session. She wanted others to believe she was a team player committed to solving the problem and making the changes that were necessary. However, her contribution wasn't about behavior or work practices but systemic changes that would be very difficult and take a long time to implement. For example, she suggested reengineering product development; restructuring the organization; and revamping goal setting, financial targets, and total rewards.

Her message was that for the problem to be solved, E&M needed to embark on a massive and complex organizational transformation. This is not to say she was wrong, as these were issues that eventually needed to be addressed, but the question asked was about what we would see people doing, not about the changes needed for this to happen. As the facilitator, I instructed that ideas involving systemic changes, while relevant, should be parked, as this would be covered later in the CASPE process. For this discussion, I said, we needed to focus on behaviors. This didn't stop Caroline. She continued to bring forward systemic issues and avoided talking about behavior. Eventually, with my encouragement, the CEO intervened to address the situation.

I mention this because it could happen in a session you are facilitating. Anticipating when dynamics like this might occur can help you plan how to handle the situation effectively. If you are wondering, Michel, the CEO, told the group they needed to focus on behavior and other changes that could be implemented within three to four months, which was a criterion for selecting the problem scenario. He then told them that anything else was out of scope, but he was open to revisiting these after this initiative was completed. The second thing he did was speak with Caroline in private at the next break. He told her that he needed her to start offering suggestions for immediate changes that were within her and the other business unit leaders' control. He then reconvened the meeting and asked if there were any other ideas or suggestions, looking pointedly at Caroline.

LAND MINE #8: LACK OF ALIGNMENT AND ACCOUNTABILITY

As the saying goes, the chain is only as strong as its weakest link. For culture change to be successful, leaders and employees must be accountable for their behavior and actions. This is especially true for leaders accountable for the change who, as we've discussed, influence others not just as role models of acceptable behavior but by creating the conditions to support these behaviors. When one or more leaders act in a manner that is not aligned with the culture the organization needs to solve the problem it is facing, they undermine the entire change effort.

In addition, alignment and consistency are necessary to achieve the cohesiveness required for people to effectively deal with complex and emerging issues. This is especially important when the leaders and other employees involved come from different groups or when there has been a history of conflict or a lack of collaboration, as was the case at E&M. In these situations, it is common for people to test leaders' commitment to the change by intentionally doing things the way they have in the past or in a manner that is at odds with what leaders say they want. If leaders fail to notice and call out this behavior, they are, in effect, condoning it.

Of course, this can happen unintentionally simply because it takes time for behaviors to change and for people to learn new habits. As a result, it is important to not make assumptions about motives and to ask questions to understand why people are behaving the way they are. In most cases, all that is needed is to tell people when they are slipping into old ways of doing things or behaving in a manner that is different than what is needed and expected. However, if the behavior is repeated, this can be a sign of resistance, which needs to be addressed by providing clear, constructive, and timely feedback.

When this involves the behavior of a leader, the accountability bar is higher, which makes feedback even more important. One strategy that can help is to build a discussion about accountability into the CASPE process, which fits best in phase two. Specifically, ask how leaders are going to hold themselves and one another accountable. This can be as simple as a commitment to tell someone when they are acting in a matter that is not consistent with the behaviors required to solve the problem. Another option is to build in a formal process through which leaders provide one another with feedback. For example, leaders could write down one thing they need to start, stop, and continue doing to model the behaviors and create the right conditions. Some organizations take this one step further and ask managers to provide leaders with feedback and employees to provide managers with feedback. There are many options. The key is to do something and do it well.

LAND MINE #9: MAKING PERSONAL DEVELOPMENT THE PRIMARY OBJECTIVE

The CASPE process is a powerful learning and development opportunity. However, this is not the primary objective, nor should it be. The primary objective is to solve an urgent business problem by changing the culture. This should determine who is involved at each stage of the process, not who would benefit from the learning experience. I raise this issue because I've seen it happen, and it is a red flag. The CASPE process works when leaders view it as a solution to a pressing problem. If they start to see it as a training program, even if it is to prepare people to use the process, they are more likely to delegate responsibility for the process to HR. While they may be involved, they won't demonstrate the personal ownership and active engagement needed for the CASPE process to succeed.

LAND MINE #10: RATHOLES AND DEAD HORSES

This land mine may seem minor in comparison to some of the others, but trust me, it can be a big problem. People, especially leaders, like to wrestle with business problems and talk about tangible things affecting work. Problem-solving is something most people working in organizations, especially leaders, enjoy and are very comfortable and confident doing. Put a group of leaders or subject matter experts in a room and give them a problem to solve and watch them go. This is great, except when it's not.

The CASPE process requires changing behavior, which is not something most people know how to do or are comfortable discussing. As a result, I often see groups attempt to dive down ratholes, meaning they revisit all the different things that have been tried in the past but have failed to solve the problem. They suggest that failure occurred because something was missed or not implemented correctly, and if this was addressed, the problem would be solved. Even more commonly, I see groups get stuck rehashing old arguments and advocating for prior points of view, leading to an endless spiral with no satisfactory conclusion.

If this happens, it needs to be firmly and quickly shut down even though people may argue that what they are saying is relevant and important. Do not get sucked in. Make it clear from the beginning that the group needs to follow the process, which means staying on topic and not rehashing old news. The reason they are here is because past efforts have failed. Revisiting history and old arguments is not productive.

THE ELEPHANT IN THE ROOM

While each of these land mines can cause a problem for the culture change effort, the bigger elephant in the room is the potential that employees will actively, or passively, resist the change. Any major transformation can feel threatening and create anxiety, especially in the early stages, when people may experience a sense of loss and the frustration that comes with a lack of control over events.[24] This is especially true of culture change, as this requires that people learn how to behave and do things differently, despite the old way of doing things having been, at least for a period of time, effective and successful. Accepting that change is needed, especially when it affects them personally, is not easy for most people. This is why it is important to be proactive and, with the understanding that resistance is likely, put plans in place to manage the people side of change.

PART THREE

ACCELERATING CULTURE CHANGE

CHAPTER ELEVEN

CHANGE IS THREATENING

CHANGES ARE IMPLEMENTED ALL the time in organizations; however, most do not involve or lead to culture change. In fact, the nature of and approach to the change and its effectiveness is either determined by the culture or limited by it. For example, let's say a company that has a process-oriented culture decides to invest in an enterprise software solution. This is a massive change requiring new skills and knowledge and affecting the way work is done. It is not, however, a culture change. In fact, the change strengthens the current process-oriented culture.

On the other hand, consider a company that has a different culture, one that isn't process-oriented but instead values flexibility and doing whatever is needed to achieve results. In this case, making the same change is 100 percent guaranteed to be met with resistance; the culture will create obstacles and limit the effectiveness of the change effort. In some cases, the culture may even sabotage the entire transformation effort. This is why it is important to consider how culture might affect the success of the change effort before undertaking any major transformation.

This is also why it is necessary to be thoughtful and intentional in your approach to culture change. Changes that require new behaviors and ways of working can be threatening and create high levels of anxiety, leading to resistance. Although the results-oriented, problem-solving approach used in the CASPE culture change process alleviates this to some extent, there are a few best practices you can employ to increase the likelihood of success. These are communication, managing the people side of change, and celebrating success.

COMMUNICATE AND THEN COMMUNICATE AGAIN . . . AND AGAIN

When an organization embarks on a major change, it is more important than ever that relevant information be shared in a timely and effective manner. We all know this, and yet, time and again, people complain that they haven't heard about or don't understand what is happening. If the change affects them, their work, or their colleagues, a lack of communication can trigger anxiety and stress, negatively affecting morale and performance and leading to resistance. This is why it is important to craft and implement a robust communication plan at the outset of the change initiative.

So, what makes a communication plan robust and effective? There are plenty of resources available in the public domain that can help answer this question in depth.[25] That said, there are a few principles that are especially important. The first is to understand your audience, in other words, the people who are affected by the change, whose support is required for the change to be successful, or who need to know about the change to gain broader buy-in and traction. With your audience identified, you can then determine the right messages and most effective ways to share them. When deciding on the message, it is important to put yourself in your audience's shoes. What is important to them? What do they want and need to know? What is the most effective way to reach them? What are their fears and concerns? How might they react to the change? What objections might they have?

Given that the CASPE process is about culture change and learning new behaviors and ways of working, the number one question you should be prepared to answer is, "How does the change affect me and my colleagues?" The second is, "What's in it for me?" There are many others as well. "How does behaving and doing things this way improve my work experience?" "Does it make my work more interesting, challenging, or rewarding?" "Will I meet new people and expand my network?" "Does it help me develop my skills and knowledge or improve my career prospects?" "Am I going to get the support and guidance I need to be successful?" These are the things people want and need to know.

Equally important are the ways you communicate and the methods you use. To be effective, use a variety of approaches, including dialogue, to build understanding, acceptance, and commitment. Whatever methods you choose, it is important to encourage two-way communication. You do this by asking questions and listening to understand the other person's perspective, not by advocating for or defending your point of view. You should also use language and examples your audience can relate to, showing them that you understand what is important to them, you care, and it isn't just you that needs to do this.

Every leader and manager who is involved in the change effort needs to engage in these conversations with the people within their sphere of influence who are affected by the change. As a reminder, a person's sphere of influence refers to the people and things (policies, processes, structures, space, and so on) directly or indirectly affected by that person's actions. This is especially important when communicating with employees, as they are likely to have a higher level of trust in their immediate manager, assuming they have a positive working relationship, than with senior leaders or others who are more removed. This trust helps to create the psychological safety necessary for people to speak openly about their concerns, offer their opinions, and make suggestions.[26] If this is a competency that is weak or lacking, consider offering training to managers. This will not only increase the likelihood of success in implementing this initiative, but it will also increase overall management effectiveness.

Communication, including dialogue, should of course continue throughout the culture change effort. At each step, the message and conversations will change; however, the objectives remain the same, which are to explain what is happening and why, build understanding and acceptance, and gather new information and insights to learn and improve. Whatever you do, be transparent, and when it is appropriate, share missteps as well as successes. Remember that no one expects everything to be perfect. Mistakes happen. Unexpected challenges surface. Things change. In fact, if everything comes across as too perfect, you could risk a credibility hit, which is something none of us needs or wants.

The more you can make the information you share and the ways you share it interesting and engaging, the better. One way to do this is to tell stories of people's experiences, the good and the bad, the humbling and the enlightening. Of course, the stories need to be authentic and resonate with the people who are listening or reading. It isn't enough to explain how a change in culture that included new ways of working solved a problem the company was facing. They want to hear from their peers and colleagues about their experience—the good, the bad, and the ugly, including the answer to the question, "What's in it for me?" If their experience and the stories you tell resonate in a positive way with employees, it can generate interest and spark curiosity. Managers and employees want to know and learn more, and better yet, they want to be involved. They want to be a part of this exciting change that is happening in the company. When this happens, you start to create a movement, which helps build the momentum required to expand and scale the change effort.

It is also important to remember that this is a culture change initiative with implications for the entire organization. This means your communication strategy and plan need to be broad and forward-looking. The pilot is just the beginning. If it is successful, the approach and solution will be applied across the organization until the business problem is solved. As a result, you want to capture the organization's attention early and build on this to gain traction when you reach step five, expand and scale.

MANAGE THE PEOPLE SIDE OF CHANGE

Culture change is a big transformation, because it affects people. Beliefs are questioned; behaviors are challenged; and the way people are used to working, sometimes for a long time, changes. It is a lot for anyone to deal with. Effective communication can go a long way in reducing employee stress and anxiety and alleviating the risk that employees will resist the change effort. However, there are other things you can do to increase the likelihood of success. One of these is to purposefully engage employees in the change effort. The design of the CASPE culture change process does this to some extent. Step three, solve the problem, engages managers and subject matter experts to validate the solution that leaders identified and determine the specific changes and actions required to make it happen. More employees will then be involved in the pilot (step four), as they participate in meetings to assess progress, problem solve, and identify lessons learned. However, as with communication, the more you engage employees in changes that affect them, the more likely they are to accept and even get excited about what is happening.

In a smaller organization, you are probably already engaging everyone on the team or teams that are affected by the change, so there is little need to do anything further. However, in larger organizations, it may not be possible to involve everyone, either because of the disruption to the business or logistical concerns regarding group size and geographic distance. If the latter is the case, it is important to find other ways to engage employees.

One way to do this is to build in additional meetings so the people who are not directly involved can contribute their expertise and offer ideas and suggestions. You can also suggest that leaders invite people to sit in on team meetings or spend a day shadowing the team. Another option is for leaders to ask a subset of team members to host forums that showcase what they are doing and share their experiences so far. Doing this at key points in the change effort can help people feel like they are part of it, if only from a distance. If this seems daunting, remember there are always external consultants you can reach out to for assistance. There are also many articles, videos, and books available if you want to learn more about designing and implementing an effective change management strategy.

CELEBRATE SUCCESS

Change is tough, especially when it involves changing behavior and ways of doing things. This is why it is important to reinforce the positives and celebrate success. Most people want to do well, put in a good day's work, and be proud of their achievements. When it comes to changing the way they behave and do things, they also want to know they are on the right track. Unfortunately, this often gets forgotten in the hustle and bustle of work. It doesn't help that most of us are wired to be critical and tend to focus on what someone's doing wrong instead of what they are doing right.

An easy yet powerful way to reinforce a new behavior is to make a habit of catching people doing something right. This doesn't need to be a big deal or take a lot of time or effort. All that is needed is for a senior leader, immediate manager, or yourself to simply tell someone that you saw them doing something the right way and that this is exactly what is needed. Thank you. Doing this not only helps the person but shows them, and others who observe this or hear about it, that you are serious about the need to change. If you can encourage everyone involved to do this, even better.

Observing and interacting with people during the pilot is a perfect opportunity to do this. In fact, this is not restricted to the pilot. There is nothing stopping you, or others for that matter, from walking around and observing people and using this time to reinforce the desired behavior and spread the word regarding the need to change. The important thing is for leaders to do this on a regular basis, especially during the pilot, and do it often. Even if it is only for ten minutes a day, simply being present and reinforcing one positive behavior can make a big difference. As an HR/OD professional, you may not have as much influence, but any encouragement can help. Also, doing so will likely lead to insights you can use to coach and advise leaders.

One thing that can help is to suggest to leaders that they schedule daily calendar reminders for sixty-six days to observe the team in action. This will create opportunities to catch people demonstrating the new behaviors and ways of working and gain firsthand information regarding the status of the change effort. Perhaps even more significant is that, in doing this, they lead by example and show others through their actions that they are actively involved and personally committed to achieving culture change. Because, as you know, culture change will not happen unless senior leaders and managers lead the way.

As for celebrating success, the objective is to instill a sense of pride in individuals and teams. While most leaders have the best of intentions when it comes to recognizing and rewarding people, this often gets lost in the barrage of things happening on any given day. One way to prevent this is to suggest they build celebrations into everyday activities and key milestones during the pilot and expand phases. These don't need to be big events. A Friday afternoon pizza party is an example. Simply taking the time to recognize people's accomplishments and, equally important, shine a spotlight on what they are doing to change the culture can be very effective, as well as something that they enjoy and look forward to. In this way, celebrating becomes a normal practice and not a single event.

In addition to rewarding outcomes and achievements, it is important to recognize and reward individuals or teams for successfully changing their behavior, even if it has yet to show results. Ideally, everyone involved in the pilot or expanded phases of the CASPE process quickly learns these behaviors and demonstrates them as they go about their work. However, if someone is an outstanding or exceptional role model for others, you can suggest the leader do something more to show appreciation for their effort and contribution. In this case, a meaningful reward such as a bonus, gift, or even paid time off given in a public setting is entirely appropriate. That said, it is important that there be rigor in determining who is to receive the rewards, as recognizing the wrong person can be damaging. One thing that can help is to watch and listen to what others say and do. Are they following the person's lead? Do they go to this person for advice or help? Do others talk about the person as a role model? The key is to avoid allowing personal preferences and biases to unduly influence the decision. Remind the leader that the purpose of formal recognition is to demonstrate appreciation for exceptional performance and, in doing so, motivate the person and others to continue to excel.

On a related note, I sometimes get asked about the use of "spot awards" to recognize behavior or outstanding effort. These are given by managers or employees to another team or individual who has done something they believe is worthy of recognition. My answer is to use all the various tools you have at your disposal, as I have rarely encountered an organization that uses too much recognition. However, it is important to put some guidelines in place, including clear criteria for giving a spot award. Typically, this includes demonstrating the new behaviors while doing something exceptional that goes above and beyond what is normally expected. Note that the emphasis is on both behavior and outcomes, not the outcomes alone. If you only focus on the outcomes, you risk that people will do whatever they believe is necessary to achieve them regardless of behavior. If this happens, it can undermine the needed culture change, which, while it might be positive in the short term, could prevent the business problem from being solved.

A FINAL WORD

Communicating, managing the people side of change, and cele-brating success can help to overcome resistance and, better yet, generate curiosity and interest. Ideally, as more and more evidence of the positive benefits for the company and employees is gathered and shared, the excitement grows, stories spread like wildfire, and change begins to happen organically. However, this can take time, and—especially in large, complex organiza-tions—a more intentional approach may be needed to build the momentum for this to happen.

CHAPTER TWELVE
BUILDING MOMENTUM

ONE OF THE MAIN concerns leaders have when considering culture change is the length of time it takes to see results. This worry is well-founded, as most traditional approaches take years to implement with no guarantee of a successful outcome. One of the advantages of the CASPE process is that it can be implemented in months, sometimes sooner, with clear outcomes at the end. However, in a large and complex organization, the initial shift is often just the tip of the iceberg. Achieving meaningful and sustainable culture change requires scaling and expanding the CASPE process, which can take years and be resource- and time-intensive. If this is the case in your organization, there are a few things you can do in conjunction with the CASPE process to help the culture change gain traction and even accelerate.

In this chapter, we look at three approaches you, as an HR/OD professional, can use to address this challenge. The first is the design of talent management processes, practices, and methods. The second is to create a network of culture champions. The third is to build training into the CASPE process.

TALENT MANAGEMENT PROCESSES, PRACTICES, AND METHODS

During the CASPE process, the need for systemic changes that fall within HR/OD's realm of responsibility is almost always identified. This includes but is not limited to performance management and total rewards, which were especially thorny issues at E&M. Another example is workforce planning and the restructuring of roles, responsibilities, and reporting relation-ships, or as in E&M's case, the structure of the entire organiza-tion. There are, however, other systemic changes you can make to embed the new behaviors into talent management policies and practices that, while not identified as barriers, can be pow-erful enablers and accelerators. This begins with championing the need to update the company's values to align with the new culture, which, though it is the responsibility of senior leaders, can easily be forgotten. It can also include updating competen-cy models to reflect and emphasize new and different behaviors and ways of working.

With the new behaviors and competencies identified, you can revise the criteria used for hiring, performance manage-ment, employee transitions, succession planning, and total rewards. For example, changes can be made by talent acqui-sition to ensure the company is hiring people whose person-alities and behaviors are aligned with the new culture. In so doing, HR helps seed the new behaviors throughout the orga-nization. Similarly, onboarding programs can be modified to help new hires understand the current culture as well as the culture the company needs to execute its strategy, the chang-es taking place and why these are important, and what that means for them personally. This prepares new employees to recognize and know how to respond to certain behaviors and other artifacts of the old culture. If this doesn't happen, there is always a risk that your new hires will adapt their behavior to fit the old culture or that they will decide to leave because of the dissonance between what they were told the culture was, their personal values, and their actual experience.

A similar logic applies to the other areas within talent management, including employee transition and succession planning. Making the new behaviors part of the decision process when determining who advances, moves into a new role, or is transitioned out of the organization is a powerful way to send the message that these behaviors are important. Designing or modifying recognition programs to bring attention to the new behaviors and their value can also be effective. The range of options is extensive and, when executed in a planned way, can accelerate the change process.

The challenge, other than the work and resources involved, is to do this in step with the CASPE process to maximize impact. In most organizations, such as E&M, these changes occurred as part of the expand and scale phase, beginning with those areas that were deemed to be of highest priority and that could be actioned in a reasonable time frame. In E&M's case, this was performance management and total rewards followed by the restructuring of roles and reporting relationships, with the intent to revisit the broader organization design question later. In parallel with this, the talent management team identified other changes to embed the new behaviors in their practices, processes, and tools, then crafted a plan to implement them in stages over the next three years. In the final plan, specific initiatives were identified for each year and in all areas of talent management. In areas that were less complex or not as large in scope, such as talent acquisition and onboarding, the plan was to implement the full change in the first year. Others, such as succession planning, were to be completed in phases.

CREATE A MOVEMENT WITH A CULTURE CHAMPIONS INITIATIVE

As I noted in chapter three, bottom-up culture change efforts, also known as grassroots movements, on their own are not very effective. This is because they fail to engage leaders to the extent that is necessary to achieve a meaningful and sustained change in culture. That said, there is value in doing things that expand employee engagement beyond the CASPE process. This is what creating a movement is about—bringing people on the change journey with you.

By definition, a grassroots movement is initiated by one or more employees whom others follow until, eventually, the movement builds to the point that it influences the decisions and actions of leaders. This happened at E&M when, unbeknownst to management, a team of engineers connected with other engineers in different parts of and outside the company to explore the potential of using AI in designing their products. By the time the managers became aware of it, the initiative had generated so much excitement and energy that they had no choice but to support it. This is a great example of exactly the sort of change that E&M wanted; however, it was an isolated situation. To gain traction, the company needed to take this concept and use it to architect a movement that would get people excited to be part of the change. The result was a culture champions initiative.

A culture champions initiative is a high-engagement strategy that is part communication and education and part problem-solving and action. To be clear, a culture champions initiative is not a series of focus groups or training programs, although these may be part of it. Focus groups are a method for gathering information, while training programs educate and teach people new things. Culture champions are change agents. They form a cross-functional, multilevel team of people who, when fully engaged and committed, lead the way and bring others with them on the culture change journey. These are the influencers who shape others' opinions and even their behavior. They provide a means to reach wide and deep into the organization, influencing more people in more places than is possible through any other method. By engaging them at the right time in the right way, we create a movement that accelerates the change process.

When a culture champions initiative is launched in concert with the CASPE process, the team members work on the same culture problem as leaders. The difference is that they focus on less urgent and smaller-scope problems, which are selected from the list identified by leaders in phase one. In addition to engaging more people, this approach builds internal culture change capability by providing the culture champions, leaders, and others involved in the initiative with firsthand knowledge and experience of what works and what doesn't. They can then take the lessons they have learned back to their teams and jobs, where they can be applied to other challenges.

It is important to remember that creating a movement is about building energy and momentum. If you must convince or mandate people to get involved, you've pretty much doomed the movement to fail. As such, the best time to launch a culture champions initiative is when there is already buzz, when employees are noticing and talking about the change and want to know more and be a part of it.

At E&M, a culture champions initiative was launched to explore how strengthening collaboration could improve business performance (efficiency and effectiveness) in areas of the business that were not involved in the pilot. From the list of problem areas identified in phase one, several were selected and assigned to culture champion teams. As part of their training, the teams attended a culture camp where they learned about the outcomes from phases one and two of the CASPE process and worked through phase three for their problem scenario. The culture camp was also attended by senior leaders, who were actively involved in the presentations, discussions, and activities. Following the first culture camp, the culture champion teams, with the assistance of an HR/OD coach facilitator and the active involvement of a senior leader sponsor, worked independently to implement phase four (action teams). Throughout phase four, the senior leader observed the team and met with them and their coach on a regular basis to discuss their progress, lessons learned, and obstacles they had encountered and provide support and guidance. The senior leaders and coaches of the different teams also met periodically to share information and problem solve. Once the teams completed their projects, they gathered with senior leaders at a second culture camp convened for the purpose of sharing lessons learned and ideas for the next phase of the culture change journey, the message being that culture change is not a onetime event.

BUILD TRAINING INTO THE CASPE PROCESS

Early in my career, I was hired by a highly respected and progressive telecommunications manufacturing company to be part of a culture change initiative. My role as an HR/OD professional was to help lead the design and delivery of a training curriculum focused on changing behavior to align with the company's values and its commitment to become a more customer-focused organization. I had no experience or background in any of this. I had been groomed to be a general manager, and my resume included management roles in several functions and departments, including finance, operations, and information technology. Notably absent was experience in human resources, including change management, learning and development, organizational development, and culture. So, why on earth did they hire me? They hired me because I understood their customers, having worked in or with almost every major telecom operator in North America. I also understood how to work with engineers, technical experts, field managers, and frontline employees. The thought was that this combination of experience meant I would make sure the learning experience would be received well by managers and employees, which had not always been the case. As for the program design and delivery, leadership figured I could tap into the expertise of people inside and outside the company. All that is to say, with a lot of help from some amazing people, we developed a values and culture training curriculum that won awards for innovation and excellence from the company and its largest customer. Yet, in the end, it did not change the culture.

The problem is, as I've said before, training initiatives on their own will not result in culture change; however, if they are well-designed and part of a broader change strategy, they can reinforce and potentially accelerate the change effort. When I have seen training programs add value to a culture change effort, they have focused on three things. The first we discussed in chapter eight, which is to increase self-awareness and behavior change at all levels, but especially for people in management and senior leadership roles. This is accompanied by ongoing feedback and coaching, which are typically provided by the person's manager and members of an accountability circle identified during the training. The second is to provide skills training to leaders and managers who are using the CASPE process. This includes skills such as facilitation, coaching, giving and receiving feedback, holding difficult conversations, and even project management. Some organizations choose to embed this training into the CASPE process, while others offer it in advance so leaders and managers are prepared when the initiative is launched. The third is to use immersive experiences that are designed for managers and employees to embody the new way of behaving and working. I saw an example of this in a company I worked with that created a "day-in-the-life" simulation where employees could see, hear, and feel what it was like to have a truly customer-focused culture. Talk about creating a buzz!

In all three of these steps, there should be a clear connection between the objectives, design, and content of the training and that of the CASPE process. For example, the behavioral training should be based on the behaviors identified in phase two (analyze the culture problem). The skills training should prepare leaders for phase three (solve the culture problem) and phase four (pilot the solution). And the immersive experiences should be built into phase five (expand and scale). When used in combination, these points of focus are very effective at building momentum for culture change; however, they do take resources to implement.

A FINAL THOUGHT

Each of these strategies on their own and in combination can help to build momentum, gain traction, and accelerate culture change. However, there is a cost in terms of time, money, and other resources that needs to be considered before embarking on any of the above. If you are forced to make a choice, my advice is to start with things that are within your control and prioritize them based on HR/OD's capacity and capabilities. Making the changes suggested to any one of the core processes mentioned will have a significant positive impact.

CHAPTER THIRTEEN

ENGAGING LEADERS, CHANGING CULTURE

CULTURE CHANGE IS HARD, period. At the same time the culture change effort is happening, the organization continues to go about its business, which typically consumes most of its available resources. This limits capacity, which means tough choices must be made. That said, if the reason for the culture change is compelling enough that the organization is willing to make the investment, then the CASPE process can make a difference.

Culture change is also a journey that takes a sustained commitment of attention, energy, and resources. It is not for the faint of heart; however, it is often the only option when old ways of doing things are no longer delivering the necessary results. Indeed, one might argue that given the increasing complexity, volatility, uncertainty, and ambiguity of today's world, companies need to constantly challenge their assumptions and beliefs to stay relevant. In other words, senior leaders must recognize when culture change is needed and have built up the muscle required to make it happen.

Yet, the biggest challenge we face as HR/OD leaders and professionals is to convince leaders, especially those in executive and other senior roles, to actively own and engage in culture change. For culture change to be successful, they must be fully committed to the change and personally involved in a meaningful way in all phases. Sure, they are going to need help, but they are going to have to lead the way, which means showing—not just telling—others what is expected, making tough decisions, and creating the conditions for success. It can't be a nice-to-do item, nor can it be delegated.

Hopefully, this book has provided you with the information, knowledge, and tools you need to do exactly that. You can sit down with leaders, show them the culture drag dynamic, and explain how culture affects strategy execution. You have stories you can draw on to make this real, or even better, you can craft your own examples using the ones provided in this book as a template. Better yet, you have practiced using the model and become so skilled that you can use it to help leaders understand how culture is contributing to their business problems and how the CASPE process can make a difference. You can explain how, as leaders, they already know how to solve complex problems. A misalignment of culture and strategy that is affecting the business is just that—a complex problem that needs to be solved. Instead of focusing on culture, the CASPE process directs attention toward solving a business problem that is caused by culture. It provides a framework for identifying the changes to behavior and the structures that encourage and support these behaviors that are necessary to solve the problem. It is practical, straightforward, and efficient. Most importantly, it works.

WHAT ABOUT CONVINCING LEADERS TO TAKE OWNERSHIP OF AND ACTIVELY ENGAGE IN THE CULTURE CHANGE EFFORT?

I've found the best approach is to not make this an up-front condition for embarking on culture change. Better yet, don't talk about their participation at all until there is something tangible to discuss. Asking leaders to embrace a role that sounds vague, time-intensive, uncomfortable, and potentially threatening without a tangible example is setting ourselves up to fail. By tangible, I mean the leader acknowledges that the current culture is a problem and they need to do something about it. They will ask for your help and guidance, at which point you must make it clear that your role is to advise and support them, but they must lead the way. To lead the way means they aren't just sponsoring the initiative; they own it. They acknowledge that changing the culture means they may need to make some changes themselves and are open to the coaching and feedback you can provide. They agree to be actively involved in the entire process and will follow your guidance regarding how to do this.

Ultimately, you should be direct and clear in contracting with the leader, especially regarding roles and expectations. If they are unwilling to make this commitment, then this is the end of the discussion. Only the leader can change the culture. You, and the rest of the HR/OD team, can help and support that person, but you cannot do it for the leader, period.

By speaking their language, using a business-driven approach, and making their role tangible, we significantly increase the probability that leaders will personally engage in culture change. The good news is that having this conversation should not be difficult. Most HR/OD professionals are used to talking about business problems, gaps, solutions, and action plans. We can't be successful without this. All we need to do is apply the same language and approach to culture.

BE THE CULTURE CHANGE AGENT YOUR ORGANIZATION NEEDS YOU TO BE

As an HR/OD leader or professional who is guiding and supporting leaders and their teams through culture change, you set the tone for how others behave. This means you must also model the new behaviors, which might mean making some personal changes. Ultimately, influencing the behaviors of others requires that you are consistent in your words and actions. It is this consistency that builds the trust needed to convince others that change is worthwhile.

If this, or anything else I have recommended or shared, seems daunting or overwhelming, remember that you are not alone. Help is available if you need it. You can start by visiting my website and browsing the articles on the resources page (culturestrategyfit.com/resources). You can also contact me through LinkedIn (linkedin.com/in/nancieevans), via my website (culturestrategyfit.com/contact), or by email (nancie@ culturestrategyfit.com). I always appreciate the opportunity to connect with people who are passionate about doing great culture work. And, of course, you can always use this book as a resource. It contains a lot of great information you can refer to when you need it.

Finally, the best advice I can give is to go for it. If your organization needs to close a culture gap, it is time to act. Change starts when one person takes the first step toward the future. That person could be you. You now have the knowledge, along with the skills you already have, to be the culture change agent your organization needs. Go for it!

ACKNOWLEDGMENTS

FOR OVER THIRTY YEARS, I have had the privilege of working with amazing men and women who are striving to be great leaders and build great teams and organizations, leaders who individually and together want to create workplaces with great cultures—places where people can be their very best while helping their organizations stand out from their competitors. This has also provided the opportunity to partner with some truly outstanding human resources professionals whose commitment to developing leaders and building great cultures is inspiring. You are what makes my work amazing, and you are the reason why, after more than thirty-five years, I love what I do. Thanks to each one of you who has made and continues to make every day special. Thanks especially to the following people.

To *Ingrid Richter*, whose unique perspective, thought-provoking questions, and wonderful sense of humor always help keep me grounded.

To *Melissa Leneis*, whose unwavering trust and partnership are something I will forever value.

To *Karen McKinney*, whose indomitable spirit and positive outlook always remind me of what is important.

And finally, to *Patti Scott*, who is always there for me in good times and bad. Thank you from the bottom of my heart!

DR. NANCIE EVANS IS A CULTURE AND LEADERSHIP EXPERT WHO partners with HR/OD leaders and professionals to align their companies' cultures and strategies to achieve business results.

Nancie began her culture journey in 1988 when she had the opportunity to play a major role in a culture change initiative at a large telecommunications company. This was just the beginning of what has become her lifelong passion—developing great leaders who create great organizations with amazing cultures. In the years that followed, she has worked with organizations across a wide range of sectors and industries, developing and refining her thinking and approach to culture change. The insights gained from this experience, combined with her deep knowledge of the relationship between leadership, strategy, and culture, have resulted in the CASPE culture change process.

Nancie has a PhD in Management Learning from Lancaster University in the UK, which was preceded by an MA in Developing Human Resources from the University of Toronto and a BSc in Human Kinesiology from the University of Waterloo. She is married and has one four-legged baby, Yofi, a Coton de Tulear, and lives in Uxbridge, Ontario in Canada with her husband of thirty-five years, Alan.

An avid horsewoman, in 2012 she was forced to retire from competition (three-day eventing and dressage) after experiencing multiple head injuries. Since then, she has taken up cycling—road and mountain—and even competed in two bike races, one in Mexico with three thousand other crazy people. The best part of the hobby? Creating lasting memories with her sister Patti as they explore the world on two wheels together. For those wondering, Alan has made it very clear he has absolutely no interest in joining them.

To learn more, please visit
https://www.culturestrategyfit.com/our-culture-guru

ENDNOTES

1   "Global Culture Survey 2021: The Link Between Culture and Competitive Advantage," PricewaterhouseCoopers, 2021, https://www.pwc.com/gx/en/issues/upskilling/global-culture-survey-2021/global-culture-survey-2021-report.html.

2   "The Wrong Ways to Strengthen Culture," Harvard Business Review, 2019, https://hbr.org/2019/07/the-wrong-ways-to-strengthen-culture.

3   Deal, Terrence E., and Allan A. Kennedy. Corporate Cultures: The Rites and Rituals of Corporate Life. Reading, MA: Addison-Wesley, 1982.

4   Graham Kenny, "Don't Make This Common M&A Mistake," Harvard Business Review, March 16, 2020, https://hbr.org/2020/03/dont-make-this-common-ma-mistake.

5   Jon R. Katzenbach, Ilona Steffen, and Caroline Kronley, "Stop Fighting Your Culture," Harvard Business Review, August 10, 2012, https://hbr.org/2012/08/how-aetna-used-its-culture-to.

6   Stephen R. Covey, The 7 Habits of Highly Effective People: Powerful Lessons in Personal Change (New York: Simon and Schuster, 2013).

7   Kate Leto, "What Can You Really Influence? Find Out by Taking a Look at Your Sphere of Influence," Kateleto. com, accessed May 20, 2023, http://www.kateleto.com/articles/sphere-of-influence.

8   Jack Kelly, "Wells Fargo Forced To Pay \$3 Billion For The Bank's Fake Account Scandal," Forbes, February 24, 2020, https://www.forbes.com/sites/jackkelly/2020/02/24/wells-fargo-forced-to-pay-3-billion-for-the-banks-fake-account-scandal/?sh=1189d59342d2.

9   Maurizio Zollo and Sidney G. Winter, "From Organizational Routines to Dynamic Capabilities" (working paper, University of Pennsylvania, 1999).

10   https://www.culturestrategyfit.com/

11   https://www.culturestrategyfit.com/.

12   John P. Kotter and James L. Heskett, Corporate Culture and Performance (New York: Free Press, 1992).

13   Scott A. Mason, "Performance-Based Planning for Hospitals." Health Care Strategic Management 18, no. 12 (December 2000): 14.

14   Mauro F. Guillén, "How Businesses Have Successfully Pivoted During the Pandemic," Harvard Business Review, July 2020, https://hbr.org/2020/07/how-businesses-have-successfully-pivoted-during-the-pandemic.

15   Ashley Pugh, "10 Business that Failed to Adapt," E-Careers, April 2018, https://www.e-careers.com/connected/10-businesses-that-failed-to-adapt.

16   "Blockbuster (retailer), Wikipedia, December 29, 2023, https://en.wikipedia.org/wiki/Blockbuster_(retailer).

17   Marguerita Chang, "BlackBerry: A Story of Constant Success & Failure," Investopedia, March 17, 2023, https://www.investopedia.com/articles/investing/062315/blackberry-story-constant-success-failure.asp#citation-16.

18   Victor Glass, "Culture Clash and the Failure of the AT&T/Time Warner Merger," Rutgers Business Review 6, no. 3 (2021): 350–65.

19   Ted Jackson, "Types of Performance Management Systems (& How Best to Use Them)," ClearPoint Strategy, April 17, 2023, https://www.clearpointstrategy.com/blog/types-of-performance-management-systems.

20   Tim Kuppler, "Edgar Schein on the Topic of Culture," Marcella Bremer, August 28, 2015, https://www.leadershipandchangemagazine.com/edgar-schein-on-culture/.

21   "The Man Who Moves a Mountain Begins by Carrying Away Small Stones," Quotespedia, accessed December 18, 2023, https://www.quotespedia.org/authors/c/confucius/the-man-who-moves-a-mountain-begins-by-carrying-away-small-stones-confucius/.

22   Judy Brown, A Leader's Guide to Reflective Practice (Bloomington, IN: Trafford Publishing, 2006).

23   James Clear, Atomic Habits: An Easy & Proven Way to Build Good Habits & Break Bad Ones (New York: Avery, 2018).

24   Elisabeth Kübler-Ross, "On Death and Dying." Bulletin of the American College of Surgeons, 60, no. 6 (June 1975): 12, 15–17, https://pubmed.ncbi.nlm.nih.gov/10323918.

25   "Communications Checklist for Change Management," Prosci, accessed December 19, 2023, https://www.prosci.com/resources/articles/communications-checklist-for-change-management.

26   Amy Gallo, "What is Psychological Safety?" Harvard Business Review, February 15, 2023, https://hbr.org/2023/02/what-is-psychological-safety.